D0886560

THE CITY MOVES WEST

The City Moves West

ECONOMIC AND INDUSTRIAL GROWTH
IN CENTRAL WEST TEXAS

ROBERT L. MARTIN

UNIVERSITY OF TEXAS PRESS AUSTIN & LONDON

330.9764
μ38c

Standard Book Number 292-78412-0
Library of Congress Catalog Card Number 72-89807
Copyright © 1969 by Robert L. Martin
All Rights Reserved
Printed by The University of Texas Printing Division, Austin
Binding by Universal Bookbindery, Inc., San Antonio

PREFACE

General histories dealing with the southwestern United States and more detailed studies of Texas usually have neglected the importance of urban development in the Southwest. This account is intended to fill part of the gap by studying a restricted area of West Texas and by tracing the economic forces that have contributed to the growth of towns in that section. Because of the complexity of the factors to be considered it has been necessary to limit the area to the sixteen counties of central West Texas. The region under consideration is roughly that between the parallels 33 degrees on the north and 31 degrees and 30 minutes on the south, the one-hundredth meridian on the east, and the Texas-New Mexico border on the west, an area of West Texas about 90 by 180 miles.

This region forms a unit for a number of reasons. Geographically it is bordered on the north by the South Plains and on the south by the Trans-Pecos. Geologically it lies mostly in the Central Basin Uplift, so that discovery of oil in one part of the area has led to exploration of other sections. Economically it forms a unit because the growth and development of the entire area have been attributable basically to one economic factor, the presence of oil.

Within the region only cities of at least 10,000 population at the time of the 1960 census have been considered.[1] Six such cities exist:

[1] The major portion of this research was completed before the publication of the 1960 Census. A seventh town in this area achieved a population of 10,000 by 1960. Andrews, county seat of Andrews County increased in population from 611 in 1940 to 3,294 in 1950 and 11,135 in 1960. The factors discussed in

MAR 24 '71

HUNT LIBRARY
CARNEGIE-MELLON UNIVERSITY

Lamesa, Dawson County; Snyder, Scurry County; Sweetwater, Nolan County; Big Spring, Howard County; Midland, Midland County; and Odessa, Ector County. All are county seats and, although usually the only town of any size in the county, are fairly representative of smaller communities in the region.

Cities, particularly in their infancy, reflect the life of the area in which they are situated. Therefore, I also deal with the region as a whole and with the counties in which these cities are located. The area has passed through three economic phases in each of which one industry has been dominant. Although the periods overlap, fairly exact terminal dates of the time of their major importance can be established. The range cattle industry and the period of the fenced ranch dominated economic life from the eighteen-seventies to about 1900; farming gained an importance in the eighteen-eighties which continued until 1930; and the oil industry caused the urban expansion between 1920 and 1960. Since the modern city did not develop in West Texas until after 1900, a major portion of the book will deal with the more recent period.

Because this analysis is intended to be an economic study of the factors that caused the urbanization of a region, social, cultural, and political factors receive little attention.[2] The urbanization of the United States has been one of the dominant movements of the post-Civil War period. The movement reached West Texas only recently and has not been previously analyzed. This work describes the city, its development and its future in central West Texas.

---

this book in connection with the growth of other towns apply equally well to Andrews. The increase in population there was almost completely the result of oil activity (U.S., Department of Commerce, Bureau of the Census, *Eighteenth Census of the United States, 1960: Population*, I, 21).

[2] See Appendix I.

ACKNOWLEDGMENTS

This work was originally presented as my doctoral dissertation at the University of Oklahoma. I am indebted to a number of people for their help, but especially to Dr. Gilbert C. Fite, Research Professor of History, under whose direction the work was done and without whose aid and advice it could not have been completed. Thanks must also be extended to the Faculty Research Committee at Texas Christian University, which provided a much-needed grant, and to the university administration, which allowed a reduction in teaching assignment. I am particularly grateful for the critical comments of Dr. Joe B. Frantz of The University of Texas on behalf of the American Association for State and Local History. The love, devotion, and patience of my wife, Daisy Martin, have also made the work possible.

CONTENTS

M A P

THE CITY MOVES WEST

MAP OF CENTRAL WEST TEXAS

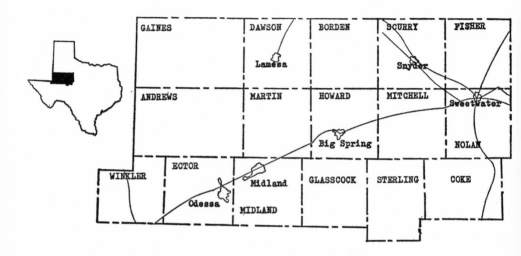

SCALE

10   0   10   20   30   40   50   60   70 MILES

CHAPTER ONE

THE CATTLE INDUSTRY

By the end of the Civil War, several million wild cattle roamed the western plains of Texas. Returning soldiers and other citizens of the state realized that a fortune was to be had by purchasing cattle from ranchers for $3.00 to $4.00 a head or, better still, by simply rounding up a herd from those that ran wild and selling them in northern markets where beef brought premium prices. It was known that the problem of transportation could be solved since Texas cattle might profitably be driven over long distances.[1]

These promising circumstances led to the founding of the range cattle industry in Texas and to the inauguration of the long drive to meet railroads pushing across Missouri and Kansas. By 1870 the industry was well-established in Texas. Grazing their herds on free public land and on privately owned ranches, cattlemen had extended the western limits of their domain to a line roughly along the ninety-eighth meridian.[2] Beyond this point there were few settlers. Although a line of forts was established in West Texas by the federal

[1] Details of the range cattle industry may be found in many works. For the general story Ernest Staples Osgood, *The Day of the Cattleman*, and Edward Everett Dale, *The Range Cattle Industry*, are standard works. In Rupert Norval Richardson, *Texas, The Lone Star State*, and William Curry Holden, *Alkali Trails, or Social and Economic Movements of the Texas Frontier, 1846–1900*, may be found accounts of the industry in Texas.

[2] Richardson, *Texas*, p. 312.

government between 1866 and 1868, Indians were still a menace to those trying to establish homes on the western plains of Texas. Protection of so long a frontier was a difficult task, and it was not until the mid-seventies that federal troops, aided by the Frontier Battalion of the Texas Rangers, were able to subdue the Indians.[3] By 1875 settlers were able to move onto the plains in relative safety.

The area then open to settlement was a vast level plain occasionally broken by undulating land, low rolling hills, or the jutting escarpment of the caprock. The soil varied from a stony clay and a fine sandy loam to rare streaks of dark waxy earth along creek beds.[4] The country was almost void of trees. A few stunted juniper, oak, and mesquite were sometimes seen, but the earth was almost everywhere covered with an abundant growth of native grasses of various types that were all highly drought-resistant.[5] A few creeks and springs provided the only surface water supply, and rainfall averaged between 22 and 16 inches annually from east to west.[6]

Rising from approximately 2,000 feet on the east to nearly 5,000 on the west, the great semiarid region was apparently an unproductive and undesirable wasteland. It did, however, possess one resource that lured the first inhabitants into the area. Large herds of buffalo grazed the native grasses of West Texas, and in the eighteen-seventies hunters began to come in from the north to take

[3] For the role of the Texas Rangers on the Texas frontier, see Walter Prescott Webb, *The Texas Rangers, A Century of Frontier Defense.*

[4] The principal soils in Nolan County are the Valera group, mostly stony clay with some clay and clay loam. In Howard, Ector, and Midland counties the main soils are Amarillo, fine sandy loams that are fairly drought-resistant. Scurry and Dawson have mainly Miles soils, fine sandy loams (Texas, Agricultural Experiment Station, *The Soils of Texas*, pp. 119–150).

[5] The native vegetation of Nolan County was largely short grasses, buffalo and various bunch grasses, and mesquite. There were many small trees in some areas, small juniper, shin oak, live oak, and shrubs. The soil in Howard, Ector, and Midland counties supported a heavy growth of natural grasses and some mesquite. The natural vegetation in Dawson and Scurry counties was bunch grasses (Texas, Agricultural Experiment Station, *Soils of Texas*, pp. 119–150).

[6] Penn Livingston and Robert R. Bennett, *Geology and Ground Water Resources of the Big Spring Area, Texas*, pp. 7–8; and D. B. Knowles, *Ground-Water Resources of Ector County, Texas*, pp. 4–5.

advantage of the presence of these animals. In 1874 the destruction of the buffalo hunters' supply base at Adobe Walls in the Texas Panhandle only temporarily held up operations. In 1875 the slaughter of the herds resumed when the Mooar brothers and others moved out from Fort Griffin to establish bases at Buffalo Gap, Hide Town, and elsewhere.[7] The Mooars had hunted buffalo in the Panhandle and in October 1876 made camp at Deep Creek, Scurry County, near Hide Town (later Snyder). There they established one of the largest outfits during the period of buffalo slaughter on the Texas plains.

After the destruction of the buffalo herds, the Mooars and many other hunters remained to establish homes, and during the same period the first ranchers moved into the area. In 1877 one of the first large ranches in Scurry County was established by the Nunn brothers, who had previously raised cattle in southern Texas.[8] In the same year Colonel C. C. Slaughter founded his cattle empire, the Lazy S Ranch, on the public domain of West Texas. At seventeen Slaughter was hauling and trading wheat and lumber in Central Texas and had managed to save a little more than $500.00, which he invested in a small herd of cattle.[9] He drove these animals to present Howard County in West Texas where a dugout in the hillside with a bullhide door provided his first ranch headquarters.[10] From these modest beginnings, Slaughter created the largest individual holding in far West Texas. His range stretched from Scurry County in the north, south into Howard County, and west to the New Mexico border, a pasture 50 miles wide and 80 miles long.[11] The Slaughter spread included land that was owned, some that was leased, and a great

[7] Holden, *Alkali Trails*, p. 60; Carl Coke Rister, *Fort Griffin on the Texas Frontier*, pp. 175–176; and Kathryn Cotten, *Saga of Scurry*, p. 10.

[8] Cotten, *Saga of Scurry*, p. 10.

[9] Lewis Nordyke, *Great Roundup, The Story of Texas and Southwestern Cowmen*, p. 19.

[10] George A. Wallis, *Cattle Kings of the Staked Plains*, p. 26.

[11] J. Marvin Hunter, ed. and comp., *The Trail Drivers of Texas*, p. 341; John Allison Rickard, "The Ranch Industry of the Texas South Plains" (Master's Thesis, University of Texas, 1927), p. 181; and Nordyke, *Great Roundup*, p. 101.

deal of the public domain on which cattle were simply grazed without charge. Slaughter bought over 200,000 acres of land from the Texas and Pacific Railroad, and in one transaction paid the line $220,485.82 for a block of land.[12] In addition, he purchased land from the state until his holdings totaled about 1,000,000 acres.[13]

Slaughter took an active interest in Texas ranching and was one of the organizers and an early president of the Texas Cattle Raisers Association.[14] The Lazy S was one of the first ranches in West Texas on which attempts were made to improve breeds of cattle. Slaughter purchased about 100 shorthorn bulls in Kentucky in the late eighteen-seventies and with them bred nearly 4,000 carefully selected longhorn heifers.[15] The experiment was apparently successful, for in 1882 he sold 1,000 three-year-old steers that averaged nearly 1,000 pounds and sold for $75.00 a head.[16]

The large area included in the Slaughter holdings was an exception in West Texas. The majority of early cattlemen had relatively small holdings and usually farmed in conjunction with raising cattle or sheep. In the late eighteen-seventies several families moved into the region, settling along the banks of creeks, and by 1880 about 1,000 people lived in central West Texas.[17] The ethnic makeup of the population then was probably much like that of ten years later when most of the residents were native born.[18]

At first few people bothered to purchase ranches because there was an abundance of free land available. As more immigrants arrived, however, an effort was made by the early settlers, especially the few ranchers who already had large holdings, to prevent new-

[12] Wallis, *Cattle Kings*, p. 27.
[13] Rickard, "Ranch Industry," p. 181.
[14] Nordyke, *Great Roundup*, p. 40.
[15] Wallis, *Cattle Kings*, p. 26; and Rickard, "Ranch Industry," p. 92.
[16] Wallis, *Cattle Kings*, p. 26.
[17] Texas, State Archives, Manuscript Census of Texas, 1880.
[18] In 1890 there were 4,070 native-born and 385 foreign-born residents in the counties under consideration. Foreign-born settlers were mainly from the British Isles and Germany, native Americans were mostly Texans. (U.S., Department of Commerce, Bureau of the Census, *Eleventh Census of the United States, 1890: Population*, I, 508–510).

comers from acquiring desirable areas. The land laws of Texas made this relatively easy, for the laws were so framed as to defeat the theory of actual residence, which was designed to attract settlers to small farms, and to make it possible for large bodies of land to be obtained.

In 1854 the Texas legislature offered sixteen alternate sections of land to railroad companies for every mile of track which was laid.[19] This practice was continued until 1882 when the Texas and Pacific crossed West Texas. Texas railroads received a total of 32,400,000 acres of land under the terms of this act.[20] The alternate sections were reserved for the public school fund, and the legislature was allowed to provide the terms of sale.

An 1874 law provided that school lands might be sold, the acreage limit being a quarter section per person and the price $1.50 an acre.[21] Since the purchaser was permitted to pay for the land over a period of several years but could obtain a patent to the land at any time after making application, the land was not reserved for actual residents, and many patentees immediately transferred their holdings to the ranchers for whom they worked. A second law in 1879 permitted an individual to buy one section of arable or three sections of pasture land.[22] This act enabled employees and friends of ranchers to apply for land actually held by the cattlemen. Two years later the minimum amount was increased to seven sections, and within a short time applications for 1,300,000 acres of land in seven-section bids were received.[23]

Although the terms of Texas land laws applied to the entire state, most of the public lands were located in West Texas. By 1884 the State Land Commissioner reported that 672,868 acres in Dawson, Howard, Scurry, and Nolan counties had been patented.[24] That

[19] Texas. Commissioner of the General Land Office, *Biennial Report,* 1908–1910, p. 29.
[20] *Ibid.*
[21] H. P. N. Gammel, ed., *General Laws of Texas,* 1822–1897, VIII, 72.
[22] *Ibid.,* IX, 55.
[23] General Land Office, *Biennial Report,* 1884–1886, p. 5.
[24] *Ibid.,* 1882–1884, p. 9.

ranchers never intended to purchase this land, but were merely hold-
ing it to keep out actual settlers, was indicated by the fact that twelve
years later 385,221 acres in the same counties had been forfeited because of failure to make the required payments.[25]

In an attempt to aid actual settlers, a state land board was created
in 1883 to direct the sale and leasing of land. A minimum price of
$2.00 an acre for land without water, $3.00 for land with water, and
$5.00 for land from which lumber could be cut was set, and acreage
was to be purchased by competitive bid.[26] No individual could buy
more than one section of pasture land; agricultural land was reserved
for actual settlers; and corporations were prohibited from making
more than one patent in a single county. Since a purchaser could sell
his land at any time after he made the first payment, the provision
restricting corporations was easily circumvented.

Unfortunately for the small farmer, the law also allowed the leasing
of land at a minimum price of $.04 an acre for a maximum period
of ten years.[27] There was little competition in the bidding, and the
minimum price was all that was obtained. In practice this act further
aided ranchers already on the scene who proceeded to lease large
areas of the more suitable acreage and thus prevented immigrants
from getting land. Under these leasing provisions C. C. Slaughter
gained control of more than 2,000,000 acres of land in West Texas
between 1884 and 1900.[28] Other large lessees in the area were the
Mooar brothers, the Rush Cattle Company, the Benson Cattle Company, the Earnest brothers, the Jumbo Cattle Company, the Alabama
and Texas Cattle Company, and the Andersen brothers. Their leased
holdings ranged from 3,000 to over 120,000 acres.[29] In February
1884, the lease price was raised to $.08 an acre, and many cattle-

[25] *Ibid.*, 1894–1896, pp. 9–10.

[26] Reuben McKitrick, "The Public Land System of Texas, 1823–1910,"
Bulletin of the University of Wisconsin, No. 905 (Madison, 1918), p. 96; and
Gammel, *General Laws of Texas*, IX, 85.

[27] General Land Office, *Biennial Report*, 1884–1886, p. 18; and Gammel,
General Laws of Texas, IX, 89.

[28] General Land Office of Texas, Land Lease Receipts, 1884–1900, Texas,
State Archives, Records Division, Austin, Texas.

[29] *Ibid.*

men refused to pay the advanced rate, demanding lease privileges at
$.04.[30]

A further weakness in the law, which once again aided ranchers,
was the provision that as leases expired the land was to be offered for
sale. Only leaseholders knew what land was to be available because
no publicity was given, and employees were used to take out patents
on areas desired by the cattlemen.[31] Moreover, ranchers who held
especially desirable land generally did not give advance notification
of their intention to let the leases lapse. To end this practice, a law of
1887, with amendments in 1889 and 1891, required the purchaser to
swear that he "desired to purchase the land for a home," and that he
was buying the land for himself.[32] Four sections, one arable and
three of pasture land, were the most that could be bought. The
purchaser was required to occupy the land for three years, and he
was given forty years to pay for it. This was an unusual example of
long-term credit being offered to those engaged in agriculture in the
nineteenth century, but did not significantly increase the number of
farmers in the area.

Subsequent laws did little to prevent the accumulation of large
landholdings. In 1895 a law was passed which, as framed, was to
yield a handsome profit to speculators. A total of 5,583,723 acres
was sold under the terms of this act, mostly as grazing land, at $1.00
an acre with 3 per cent interest on the unpaid balance.[33] The leg-
islation gave purchasers who had forfeited land under previous laws
ninety days prior right to repurchase under the new act. Thus, former
purchasers who had not paid principal or interest on $3.00-an-acre
purchases and had let the land be forfeited could now buy it back
at $1.00 with a reduced rate of interest.[34] A 1901 act gave the lessee
who had made improvements and was an actual resident a sixty-day
option to buy the land when his lease expired.[35] By constructing a

[30] General Land Office, *Biennial Report*, 1884–1886, p. 18.
[31] *Ibid.*, 1910–1912, p. 26.
[32] Gammel, *General Laws of Texas*, IX, 85.
[33] General Land Office, *Biennial Report*, 1896–1898, pp. 11–12.
[34] *Ibid.*, 1900–1902, p. 55.
[35] Gammel, *General Laws of Texas*, X, 43.

shack and using others as "residents," the ranchers were still able to increase their holdings. Charles Logan, State Land Commissioner, said in his 1902 *Biennial Report* that

The laws of 1895, 1897, and 1901 are full of contradictions and incon-sistencies. . . . While the laws were enacted ostensibly for the benefit of the actual settler, he derived but little benefit from them. The chief benefi-ciaries have been the land agents, speculators, and bonus hunters, and finally the ranch men.[36]

Certainly ranchers took advantage of the many loopholes in the laws to increase their holdings in West Texas. In 1896, over 550,000 acres of land in Dawson, Ector, Howard, Midland, Nolan, and Scurry counties were under lease, and two years later this figure had increased to more than 1,000,000 acres.[37] However, as the im-portance of farming gradually increased and that of ranching de-clined, land was sold to actual residents and the number of leases was reduced. By 1902 there still remained 585,730 acres unsold in the six counties, but in 1904 there were less than 300,000 acres avail-able, and by 1912, only 1,825 acres still remained on the market.[38] The size of individual holdings was also decreasing during this period. In 1917 the largest acreage owned by one person in each of the six counties was: Ector, 103,947; Dawson, 59,713; Howard, 22,400; Midland, 82,075; Nolan, 26,123; and Scurry, 47,386.[39] The largest ranches were to be found in the two westernmost counties where ranching was still of greater importance than farming.

Although a final land law in 1905 provided for sealed competitive bids from purchasers of land, the problem of making acreage avail-able to settlers was never satisfactorily solved.[40] Texas land laws, especially those concerning the leasing of public school lands, favored the acquisition of large holdings by cattlemen and specu-lators. The first ranchers in the area, however, were little concerned

[36] General Land Office, *Biennial Report*, 1900–1902, p. 52.
[37] *Ibid.*, 1894–1896, pp. 13–14; and 1896–1898, pp. 26–27.
[38] *Ibid.*, 1900–1902, pp. 66–68; and 1910–1912, p. 35.
[39] *Ibid.*, 1914–1916, pp. 20–23.
[40] *Ibid.*, 1914–1916, p. 42.

with the problem of competition over acreage. They simply grazed their herds on the open range.

Both cattle and sheep ranches were begun in the early eighteen-eighties. In 1880 Joel Rice started a sheep ranch fourteen miles southwest of Big Spring, Howard County, near a Texas Ranger camp.[41] The ranch, the Lucien Wells, was sold to Pierce and Hilburn in 1887 and was turned into a cattle outfit. Another sheep ranch, operated by a man named McDowell, existed in the same area from 1884 to 1893.[42] Farther to the west, in Midland County, John Scharbauer raised sheep until 1888 when he switched to cattle.[43] Even though a number of sheep ranches existed in West Texas during the early days of settlement, cattle raising was always the more important industry.

Cattlemen on the Texas plains used both the long drive and the railroad to transport their cattle to market. Although the Texas and Pacific Railroad reached the area in 1881 and 1882, the trails leading north were used extensively, and many difficulties were encountered by ranchers on the long drive. In 1884 farmers and ranchers of Kansas organized in opposition to Texas cattle being driven into the southern part of their state. They issued a manifesto that no southern trail herds would be allowed to enter Kansas that year and enforced their ban by meeting the trail herds at the border of Barber County, Kansas, armed with rifles.[44] The reason given for this order was fear of Texas steers infecting native herds with the Spanish or Texas fever that was common among southern cattle. In 1885 the Kansas legislature passed a law forbidding the introduction of Texas cattle into the state, and in the same year Colorado legislators enacted provisions that all cattle from regions south of 36 degrees latitude must be held in quarantine for sixty days in Indian Territory.[45]

Indian Territory cattlemen also expressed fear, and an association

[41] Rickard, "Ranch Industry," pp. 86–87, 164.
[42] *Ibid.*, p. 87.
[43] *Ibid.*; and Nordyke, *Great Roundup*, p. 103.
[44] Holden, *Alkali Trails*, p. 40.
[45] *Taylor County* (Texas) *News*, April 3, 1885, and July 17, 1885; and William Bennett Bizzell, *Rural Texas*, pp. 133–134.

of Cherokee Strip cattle raisers announced that they would use every means possible to oppose passage of Texas cattle through their ranges.[46] Once again the dreaded Texas fever was the reason given for this action. Actually, the danger of the disease was probably exaggerated; it was the competition of southern cattle in the Kansas market that inspired much of the opposition.

Rustlers also menaced the cattlemen's prosperity, stealing cattle both from the open range and from herds along the trails. The Texas Cattle Raisers Association took an active part in efforts to stop rustling.[47] Inspectors paid by the organization were stationed at stopping points en route to market, when cattle were unloaded to be watered, and also at the principal markets.[48] Each inspector was provided with a brand book, and rewards were offered for the apprehension and conviction of thieves. This method was so successful that in 1886 the life of Sam Calhoun, attorney for the association, was threatened as a warning to the organization.[49] Between 1883 and 1895 the Cattle Raisers Association recovered 19,411 head of cattle stolen from ranchers, but the problem of rustlers was never completely solved.[50]

A final, and ultimately fatal, threat to the long drive from Texas came from farmers moving farther out onto the plains of Kansas and Texas. As more and more land came under cultivation, ranchers faced ever-increasing difficulties in getting their cattle to market. They were sometimes met by armed farmers who refused to allow the herds to be driven across their land. Trails farther to the west were

[46] *Taylor County News*, July 3, 1885.

[47] On February 15, 1877, a group of cattlemen met at Graham, Young County. They had been notified by letter, word of mouth, and in advertisements in the few existing newspapers to meet so that joint action on the part of stock raisers might be considered. The result of the meeting was the formation of the Texas Cattle Raisers Association (Rickard, "Ranch Industry," p. 56; and Nordyke, *Great Roundup*, pp. 17–18).

[48] Rickard, "Ranch Industry," p. 56; and Louise Bradford, "A History of Nolan County, Texas" (Master's Thesis, University of Texas, 1934), p. 86.

[49] Bradford, "History of Nolan County," p. 86.

[50] James Cox, *Historical and Biographical Record of the Cattle Industry and the Cattlemen of Texas and Adjacent Territory*, pp. 226–227, 231–232.

used, and eventually the railroad became the chief shipping agent for Texas cattle.

By the mid eighteen-eighties the cattle industry of the open range was coming to an end on the Texas plains, and fenced ranges were beginning to appear. The first fences built in the early eighties were drift fences, sometimes 30 to 40 miles long, designed to prevent cattle from drifting from the range.[51] Opponents of fencing included both a large number of farmers and also a few big ranchers who owned no land and ran their cattle on the open range.

Farmers objected strongly to overambitious fencers who set up mile after mile of barbed wire without gates. On occasion roads were cut off, and towns were made inaccessible by long stretches of fences.[52] In 1883 the Texas Greenback Party encouraged resistance to fencing as a symbol of monopoly that sought to "convert small stockmen into serfs."[53] It was large ranchers who took the initiative to eliminate fencing, however; for these men were accustomed to grazing their herds without buying, and sometimes without leasing, an acre of land and were determined to continue the practice. They considered free grass and access to water inherent rights of the stockman that the legislature was bound to protect. Since no laws supporting these rights were in existence, and none were passed, it was inevitable that wire cutting would result.[54]

Ranchers who fenced were better organized, and in 1883 the Texas Livestock Association petitioned the legislature to pass a law to prevent wire cutting. A special session of the legislature was called by Governor John Ireland in January 1884, and the resulting law made wire cutting a felony.[55] The enemies of fences also received some satisfaction, for the law required the spacing of gates every

[51] Rickard, "Ranch Industry," p. 79.

[52] Wayne Gard, "The Fence Cutters," *Southwestern Historical Quarterly*, LI (July, 1947), 4.

[53] *Ibid.*, p. 3.

[54] R. D. Holt, "The Introduction of Barbed Wire Into Texas, and the Fence Cutting War," *West Texas Historical Association Yearbook*, VI (June, 1930), 65–79.

[55] Gammel, *General Laws of Texas*, IX, 34, 37.

HUNT LIBRARY
CARNEGIE-MELLON UNIVERSITY

three miles in fences of any great length and prohibited the enclosing of land not owned or leased.

Natural forces also threatened West Texas ranching in the mid-eighties. Rains in the spring of 1885 were fairly plentiful, and cattlemen were anticipating a profitable year, but in June the rains ended. By January 1886 surface water began to give out in some places, and the winter of 1885–1886 was a severe one on the plains.[56] The herds weathered the winter well, however, and in February losses were reported to be from 1 to 5 per cent, probably not more than normal losses for the winter, and the stock was still in good condition.[57]

By May 1886, however, the drought began to show all its blighting effects as the dry land cracked and the early grass withered and died. Railroads ran extra cars with large water tanks from which water was sold by the bucket or the barrel.[58] There was still some hope that the dry spell would be broken, but the summer of 1886 passed without rain and the less hardy settlers began to move back east. The drought finally ended when general rains began to fall in April and May 1887.[59] The twenty-three months without rain in 1885–1887 was a landmark in the history of West Texas.

The two years following 1887 were not very profitable for cattlemen on the West Texas plains as they tried to rebuild their herds, but by the spring of 1890 they were optimistic about the future. Then, in the latter part of March, a blizzard swept across West Texas killing many cattle. Again in 1891 a late blizzard proved disastrous to ranchers because losses of stock in some sections ran as high as 20 per cent.[60]

While the blighting effects of such forces as the drought of 1885–1887 and the blizzards of 1890 and 1891 were only temporary, a permanent threat to ranching was the ever-advancing farmer's fron-

[56] *Taylor County News*, January 22, 1886.

[57] *Ibid.*, February 26, 1886.

[58] Holden, *Alkali Trails*, p. 129.

[59] J. W. Williams, "A Statistical Study of the Drought of 1886," *West Texas Historical Association Yearbook*, XX, (October 1944), 85–109.

[60] *Taylor County News*, April 3, 1891.

tier. As the farmer approached, with his constant need for land, ranchers either sold their holdings or moved operations farther west. The westernmost area of Texas was to be the last stand for the open range industry, for here the land was thought to be unsuitable for farming. Even with the pressure from farmers, the movement of ranchers into this western section was slow. As late as 1899 only a few stockmen had moved as far west as Ector County, and there were no ranches beyond Odessa.[61] By 1895 the large ranches of West Texas had reached their greatest stage of development, and from that time on stock raising gradually declined as farming became more and more important.

The reign of the cattle barons on the West Texas plains was a fairly short one. Although they dominated the area while ranching was at its peak, they lost control quickly once farmers began to move into the region. Large-scale ranching in West Texas was an expensive proposition; consequently, most people in the region farmed in addition to raising a few cattle. The 1880 census listed most residents as farmers and stockmen or herdsmen.[62] As late as 1899 there were still nearly 150,000 cattle on ranches in the area, but farming was beginning to come into its own.[63] Indeed, some ranchers contributed to the destruction of the cattle empire by trying to raise crops on their land and thus proving that farming in the area was possible. For a few years ranching and farming held positions of nearly equal economic importance in the region, but by the turn of the century farming was beginning to overtake stock raising. During the first two decades of the twentieth century crop raising had, except in the westernmost counties, largely supplanted cattle raising in importance.

[61] Bureau of Business Research, University of Texas, *An Economic Survey of Ector County*, 1.0301–1.0302.

[62] Manuscript Census of Texas, 1880, Texas, State Archives, Austin, Texas.

[63] Although ranches did exist, no figures are available for Dawson County because it was not organized until 1905. The number of cattle in the other counties was: Ector, 21,285; Nolan, 20,270; Scurry, 25,753; Howard, 26,539; and Midland, 18,847. There were about 10,000 sheep in the entire area (Texas, Department of Agriculture, *Year Book, 1909*, pp. 137–172).

THE FIRST SETTLEMENTS

WITH THE CATTLEMEN came the first farmers and tradesmen, and the founding of settlements and organization of counties occurred while the ranching industry was being established. A legislative act of August 21, 1875, created 56 counties in West Texas, among them Dawson, Nolan, Scurry, and Howard counties.[1] Since there were few residents at the time, the latter were at first attached to other counties for administrative and judicial purposes.

Nolan County was the first of this group to be organized. In 1880 Tom Robard, a teacher, circulated a petition proposing an election for separate county officials.[2] The Shackleford County Court, to which Nolan County was attached, approved, and the election was held December 20, 1880. Despite the objections of cattlemen, who did not favor the proposal for fear of higher taxes and restrictions on the movement of their herds if a county government were close at hand, the election carried.[3]

Howard County, when created, was attached to Mitchell County for judicial purposes. In August 1882, the county was organized

[1] H. P. N. Gammel, General Laws of Texas, 1822–1897, VIII, 238–239.

[2] Texas counties were at first named for those who died at the Alamo and later for any "Texas hero." Nolan County was named for Philip Nolan, "the great pioneer and scout who explored Texas in 1800" (Louise Bradford, "A History of Nolan County Texas" [Master's Thesis, University of Texas, 1934], pp. 1, 25–26).

[3] Ibid., p. 27.

and separate county officials were elected. These officers received no great financial reward for their services, for the county judge and county commissioners were paid $3.00 for each day that they were actually on duty.[4] Dawson County was attached to Howard County after the latter was organized and remained unorganized until 1905.[5] Scurry County, also created by the act of 1875 and attached to Shackleford County Court, was not separately organized until 1884 when the electorate approved such a move.[6]

The final counties to be considered, Midland and Ector, were originally included in Tom Green County. On February 26, 1886, the Texas legislature divided the western part of Tom Green County into six new counties, among them Midland and Ector.[7] Midland County, the more populous of the two, was organized almost immediately in 1886. Ector County remained unorganized and was attached to Midland for judicial purposes until 1891, when it achieved separate organization.

At the time of the creation of the fifty-six counties in 1875 there were already a few settlers in West Texas. Snyder was a small camp on Deep Creek in Scurry County where William Henry "Pete" Snyder had a trading post and engaged in the buffalo hide trade.[8] In 1881

[4] Howard County was named for Volney E. Howard, a member of the first Constitutional Convention in Texas (John R. Hutto, *Howard County in the Making*, no page).

[5] Dawson County was named for Captain Nicholas Mosby Dawson who fought at the Battle of San Jacinto (Bureau of Business Research, University of Texas, *An Economic Survey of Dawson County*, 1.03).

[6] Scurry County was named for General William R. Scurry, a member of the last Congress of the Republic of Texas (*ibid.*, 1.0203).

[7] Ector County was named in honor of General Matt Ector (Texas, Department of Agriculture, *First Annual Report of the Agricultural Bureau of the Department of Agriculture, Insurance, Statistics, and History*, 1887–1888, p. 50; the first of these reports covers 1887, and one was printed each year through 1895). Midland County was named because it was midway between Fort Worth and El Paso.

[8] Kathryn Cotten, *Saga of Scurry*, p. 6; and Carl Coke Rister, *Fort Griffin on the Texas Frontier*, p. 177. The 1880 census showed William Snyder as a storekeeper on Deep Creek, Scurry County (Manuscript Census of Texas, 1880, Texas, State Archives, Austin, Texas).

he sold his store and moved farther west to Mitchell County, but by this time other settlers had arrived on the banks of Deep Creek. After the buffalo herds were slaughtered, J. Wright Mooar and his brother had established a ranch west of Snyder about 1880.[9] In 1877 John C. Webb, a stock raiser, brought his family to Hide Town where they lived for a short time in a dugout and later in a house made of buffalo hides.[10] Within two years of his arrival from South Texas, Webb constructed one of the first wooden houses in the community.

The 1880 census reported only 102 people living in Scurry County.[11] Seven years later there were nearly 450 inhabitants in the county, the majority of them living in Snyder, which boasted five lawyers, one doctor, and four merchants to serve the needs of the people.[12] The county's only school enrolled 134 pupils who were instructed by two teachers. An evidence of permanence in the Snyder settlement was a new $20,000 courthouse, which was being constructed in 1887.[13] Scurry County population rose to 1,404 by 1890, and the census of that year reported 500 people living in the town of Snyder.[14] Since there was little immigration to West Texas during this period, the population of the county rose slowly and in 1895 was estimated to be only 1,700. By 1890 there were two schools and five teachers, and five years later thirteen schools with only twelve teachers served the needs of 399 pupils.[15] The first bank in the county, a private institution with capital of $18,000, was established about 1890, but by 1893 there were two private banks with a total capital of $80,000.[16]

---

[9] Cotten, *Saga of Scurry*, pp. 5–6; William Curry Holden, *Alkali Trails, or Social and Economic Movements of the Texas Frontier, 1846–1900*, p. 10; and Rister, *Fort Griffin*, pp. 175–176.

[10] Cotten, *Saga of Scurry*, p. 9.

[11] U.S., Department of Commerce, Bureau of the Census, *Tenth Census of the United States, 1880: Population*, V, p. 664.

[12] *First Annual Report of the Agricultural Bureau*, pp. 53, 200.

[13] *Taylor County* (Texas) *News*, October 10, 1887.

[14] *Eleventh Census of the United States, 1890: Population*, I, 510.

[15] *Ninth Annual Report of the Agricultural Bureau*, p. 231.

[16] *Seventh Annual Report of the Agricultural Bureau*, p. 433.

There was substantial expansion of trade and business in the first part of the fifteen-year period between 1880 and 1895 in Scurry County. The four mercantile establishments in 1887 increased to twelve in 1890, including two retail liquor dealers, and the number then remained relatively steady during the remainder of the period.[17] The only notable addition to the business life of the community was a cotton gin, built about 1890, which provided local ginning facilities for the few cotton raisers of the county.[18]

Economic progress in Scurry County was fairly substantial during these fifteen years. Property evaluations rose gradually from $86,620 in 1880 to $1,179,228 in 1886, fell back during two years of drought, hit a peak of $1,884,954 in 1892, and stood at $1,370,752 in 1895.[19] Almost all this property was either in land or in livestock. Land values advanced little during this fifteen-year span, standing almost unchanged at $7.00 to $15.00 an acre for improved land and $2.00 to $6.00 an acre for unimproved land.[20] An ever-increasing portion of this land was mortgaged, the average debt per acre from 1880 to 1889 being $1.60. With very few, if any, exceptions, these mortgages were held locally and were fairly equally divided between banks and merchants.[21]

County finances during the period were in a little better condition than those of individual residents. The bonded indebtedness of the county was $17,300 from 1891 to 1895, but the tax rate decreased during the same years from $.975 per $100.00 valuation to $.62 per $100.00.[22] The principal expenditure of the county was for the new courthouse, the only other public property being school buildings valued at only about $3,000.[23] Although relatively little development was evident in Scurry County, the population of the county and its

[17] *Fourth* through *Ninth Annual Reports of the Agricultural Bureau.*

[18] *Ninth Annual Report of the Agricultural Bureau,* p. 131.

[19] Tax Assessor's Rolls for Scurry County, 1880–1895, Texas, State Archives, Records Division, Austin, Texas.

[20] *First* through *Ninth Annual Reports of the Agricultural Bureau.*

[21] *Eleventh Census of the United States, 1890: Population,* I, 150, 676.

[22] *Fourth* through *Ninth Annual Reports of the Agricultural Bureau.* These reports cover the years 1891 to 1895 inclusive.

[23] *Ninth Annual Report of the Agricultural Bureau,* p. 231.

county seat, Snyder, was slowly growing, and business was on a fairly sound footing by 1895.

South of Scurry County the area was settled a little more rapidly because of the presence of the Texas and Pacific Railroad, which acted as a stimulant to immigration. The railroad reached Sweetwater, county seat of Nolan County, on March 12, 1881, and arrived at Big Spring, county seat of Howard County, May 28 of the same year.[24] In both towns celebrations were held, and citizens of the towns lined the tracks to see the engine puff into the station. Not only did the railroad provide easy access to West Texas, but also the Texas and Pacific had a great deal of land that it was eager to sell to prospective settlers. Of the 5,491,702 acres received and located by the Texas and Pacific before March 31, 1881, all but 40,383 acres were west of Fort Worth, and much of the land lay in central West Texas.[25] The railroad offered less than liberal terms to settlers, requiring one-fifth of the purchase price as a down payment and charging 8 per cent interest on the unpaid balance, which was due in four equal payments; however, the company did offer a 25 per cent discount for cash purchases.[26] An average of $3.81 was received by the railroad for the land it sold in Texas as compared with state-owned land available during the same period at $1.00 to $3.00 an acre.[27]

As early as 1874 the Texas and Pacific organized the Southwestern Immigration Company to encourage immigration to the area along the railroad route through a number of pamphlets.[28] The company's propaganda was primarily directed to the farmer, who generally had little money, because it stressed the large amount of capital required to begin ranching on the Texas Plains. The company writers were

[24] S. B. McAllister, "Building the Texas and Pacific Railroad West of Fort Worth," *West Texas Historical Association Year Book*, IV (June, 1928), 18.

[25] Millicent Seay Huff, "A Study of Work Done by Texas Railroad Companies to Encourage Immigration into Texas between 1870 and 1890" (Master's Thesis, University of Texas, 1955), p. 27.

[26] *Ibid.*, p. 29.

[27] Not only was state land cheaper in most cases, but also less interest was charged by the state on the unpaid balance (*ibid.*).

[28] Huff, "A Study of Work Done by Railroad Companies," p. 61.

sometimes less than truthful in reporting the productive capabilities of West Texas soil, but they did recommend dry farming to prospective settlers.[29] An appeal was also made to unmarried women. In an 1884 pamphlet it was predicted that Miss Carrie Schuch of Oskaloosa, Iowa, would probably "marry a million dollar ranchman before she returns" from Big Spring where she was visiting her brother, "for that is usually the destiny of attractive young ladies in this country."[30] More practical work toward the encouragement of immigration was done by the Texas and Pacific in constructing the Immigrant's Home in 1890 at Baird, Callahan County, in the heart of the land for sale.[31] From this headquarters prospective settlers were taken to view various tracts of land. That the presence of the railroad was an encouragement to immigration was evident, for Big Spring, Midland, Odessa, and Sweetwater were all settled more quickly than they normally would have been had the railroad not gone through them.

When the Texas and Pacific passed Sweetwater, Nolan County, in 1881, there were already a few settlers at the site. The first settler at present Sweetwater was probably Tom Knight, who came down from Buffalo Gap during the days of the buffalo hunt and established a store and trading post in a dugout beside Sweetwater Creek.[32] About 1879 James Manning, deputy district surveyor for Shackleford County, opened a second store as other people began to move to

[29] One pamphlet said that West Texas "soil when properly managed has remarkable resistance to drought. If it be plowed deep and the surface is frequently worked, so as to prevent the formation of a crust, crops will make a very good report of themselves with very little rain. If a crust is not permitted to form, these fat carbonaceous soils will drink enough moisture from the night air to keep crops in good condition" (Southwestern Immigration Company, *Texas: Her Resources and Capabilities,* p. 12).

[30] Huff, "A Study of Work Done by Railroad Companies," p. 41.

[31] *Ibid.,* p. 39.

[32] *Abilene* (Texas) *Reporter News,* July 18, 1953. A local historian called this first settler Billie Knight and reported him in the area in 1877 (R. C. Crane, "Early Days in Sweetwater," *West Texas Historical Association Year Book,* VIII [June, 1932], 97).

the vicinity of the creek,[33] and in the same year the citizens of the small community petitioned the government for a post office.[34] In 1880 when Nolan County was organized 640 people were settled along the banks of small streams that drained the area,[35] and in 1881 Sweetwater was declared the permanent county seat. At the time the small town was a settlement of tents without a building of stone, wood, or brick.[36] Shortly after the arrival of the railroad, lumber for homes became available because the Dulaney brothers, proprietors of a store in the town, obtained a shipment of building materials; by 1882 a few wooden houses began to replace the tents.[37]

Nearly all the first settlers were farmers and stock raisers, and a majority of the property they owned was in cattle and land.[38] To eliminate this uniformity of occupation two efforts were made during the early period of settlement to provide other means of livelihood for the people of Nolan County. In 1882 the Franco-Texan Land Company, which had extensive holdings in the county, sent G. F. Shiflett to Sweetwater to build and manage a gypsum plant for the production of plaster of Paris.[39] The purpose of the enterprise was evidently the creation of jobs to stimulate immigration, for a number of French families were brought to work in the factory. In the spring of 1882 the establishment was completed at a cost of $20,000, but the business failed within six months. In 1890 a second, similarly

[33] Crane, "Early Days in Sweetwater," p. 101; and Louis J. Wortham, *A History of Texas*, V, 305.

[34] Bradford, "History of Nolan County," p. 26.

[35] Manuscript Census of Texas, 1880, Texas, State Archives, Austin, Texas.

[36] Bradford, "History of Nolan County," p. 66. The land on which the town was built was purchased from the Franco-Texan Land Company for $1,060 (Crane, "Early Days in Sweetwater," p. 101).

[37] Bradford, "History of Nolan County," p. 66; and Bureau of Business Research, University of Texas, *An Economic Survey of Nolan County*, 1.0102.

[38] Except for a few merchants who had some property in goods and wares, the residents of Nolan County reported little property other than land and livestock until after 1900 (Tax Assessor's Roll for Nolan County, 1879–1900, Texas, State Archives, Records Division, Austin, Texas).

[39] Shiflett also managed a saloon in Sweetwater. He was killed during an argument at the establishment, and after his death the plaster of Paris project lacked leadership (Bradford, "History of Nolan County," p. 55).

unsuccessful, venture was undertaken by a Methodist minister named Hodge.[40] A movement was instigated by Hodge to build a tannery on Sweetwater Creek. He had discovered a wild plant with which the leather was to be treated for tanning, and he thought that by using this local vegetation and labor from surrounding farms a profitable business might be organized. Stock was sold to the townspeople and the plant opened, only to close again in a few months.

Other early business failures included newspapers and a bank. A newspaper, the *Sweetwater Advance,* was optimistically launched by C. E. Gilbert in 1882.[41] It became the *Nolan County Record* the same year and managed to continue publication until 1890 when it went out of business.[42] A bank, organized by Thomas Trammell in 1883 with a capital of $15,000,[43] lasted one year past the Panic of 1907 and then failed as had many other ventures.

Although there were business failures and wildcat schemes in Nolan County during its early days, the county and the town of Sweetwater developed gradually in the period between 1880 and 1895. Evidence of this growth was demonstrated in the tax evaluations during the period. In 1879 the total value of property in the county was only $31,659.[44] Evaluations rose steadily, reaching a peak of $2,561,679 in 1891, and then fell back during the years following the Panic of 1893 to stand at $1,754,998 in 1895.[45] The principal property continued to be land and cattle, with town lots in Sweetwater acquiring more value as the town grew.

The financial picture of the county compared favorably with that of other counties in the area. In 1891 the total county debt was $38,755 with a tax rate of $.60 per $100.00.[46] Four years later the

[40] *Ibid.,* p. 57.

[41] Bureau of Business Research, University of Texas, *An Economic Survey of Nolan County,* 1.02031.

[42] *Ibid.*

[43] Tax Assessor's Roll for Nolan County, 1883, Texas, State Archives, Records Division, Austin, Texas. Trammell was one of the leading pioneer businessmen in the town.

[44] *Ibid.,* 1879.

[45] *Ibid.,* 1880–1895.

[46] *Fifth Annual Report of the Agricultural Bureau,* p. 378.

debt had been reduced by $4,000, and the tax rate raised to $.65 per $100.00.[47] Real-estate mortgages remained at low figures after 1882 when the total for the county was $166,663, and for the years from 1880 to 1889 the average was $1.33 per acre.[48] Land values changed very little during this period when the first permanent settlements were being made. In 1887 land was priced at $1.00 to $5.00 an acre if unimproved and at $5.00 to $15.00 if improvements had been made.[49] By 1895 these figures had risen to between $1.00 and $6.00 and $5.00 and $20.00 respectively.[50]

The population of the county reached 1,148 in 1887, was 1,572 three years later, and was estimated to be 3,000 in 1895.[51] At that time there were three small communities in the county, Sweetwater with a population of 800, Roscoe with 300, and Hilton with 100 people.[52] The first school in the county was built on Fish Creek in 1884 and was taught by Tom Robard.[53] By 1892 there were eight schools and thirteen teachers for the 379 pupils in Nolan County.[54]

Economic progress in towns appeared to be a little more rapid than in less populated areas, for as early as 1887 the county reported having nine mercantile establishments, seven lawyers, and two physicians.[55] Eight years later there were ten lawyers, three doctors, one dentist, sixteen merchants, not counting two liquor dealers, and a flour mill located in Nolan County.[56]

The presence of the liquor stores in 1895 indicated that a temperance movement of the eighties had been unsuccessful. In 1886 the

[47] *Ninth Annual Report of the Agricultural Bureau*, p. 378.

[48] *Eleventh Census of the United States, 1890: Report of Real Estate Mortgages*, pp. 150, 672.

[49] *First Annual Report of the Agricultural Bureau*, p. 169.

[50] *Ninth Annual Report of the Agricultural Bureau*, p. 201.

[51] *First Annual Report of the Agricultural Bureau*, p. 52; *Eleventh Census of the United States, 1890: Population*, I, 510; and *Ninth Annual Report of the Agricultural Bureau*, p. 201.

[52] *Ninth Annual Report of the Agricultural Bureau*, p. 201.

[53] Bradford, "History of Nolan County," p. 88.

[54] *Sixth Annual Report of the Agricultural Bureau*, p. 250.

[55] *First Annual Report of the Agricultural Bureau*, p. 169.

[56] *Ninth Annual Report of the Agricultural Bureau*, p. 201.

Taylor County News reported that in Nolan County the "Temperance ball is still rolling, and at every turn it gains in numbers and strength, and Sweetwater will soon be noted for its sobriety."[57] Apparently the movement was not as strong as the editor thought, for in 1890 there were still two retail liquor dealers and one retail beer store doing business in the county.[58]

The presence of the Texas and Pacific Railroad and of a fairly abundant water supply from Sweetwater Creek assured the permanence and growth of the county seat in an area where transportation and an adequate water source were necessary for existence. The town early became a shipping point for cattlemen and farmers of the county in addition to being the chief trading center for Nolan County residents.

West of Nolan County, Big Spring in Howard County also received a stimulus from the arrival of the Texas and Pacific. In 1880 there were only 50 people in Howard County, 30 of whom were members of a Texas Ranger Company of the Frontier Battalion stationed in the area to guard the frontier.[59] A few ranchers, Joel Rice, the Earnest brothers, and W. T. Roberts, had moved into the county in the late seventies from other parts of Texas in search of free grass,[60] but until the railroad reached the area there was little reason for settlers to push so far west.

The slaughter of the buffalo herds had left in its wake bleached bones dotting the West Texas Plains. Residents of Howard County prepared for the arrival of the railroad by gathering these bones in great piles to be shipped out to fertilizer companies.[61] By this means early settlers could often make enough money to purchase lumber for houses.

More important than buffalo bones was the presence of water in the area. That an adequate supply of water was available at the Big

[57] *Taylor County* (Texas) *News*, February 19, 1886.

[58] *Third Annual Report of the Agricultural Bureau*, p. 188.

[59] Manuscript Census of Texas, 1880, Texas, State Archives, Austin, Texas.

[60] John R. Hutto, "Big Spring and Vicinity," *West Texas Historical Association Year Book*, VIII (June, 1932), 77.

[61] John R. Hutto, *Howard County in the Making*, no page; and Holden, *Alkali Trails*, p. 16.

Spring in Howard County had been known since 1849 when Captain Randolph B. Marcy reported its presence.[62] The site was used as headquarters for both buffalo hunters and Texas Ranger companies, and in the eighteen-seventies a few ranchers moved into the area near the spring. The first actual settlement began with the arrival of the Texas and Pacific Railroad in 1881 when men on the construction crew settled near the spring. In that year John Birdwell opened the first commercial establishment on the future townsite when his saloon began to supply liquor for the railroad crew.[63] One year later a store was opened by J. and W. Fisher, "The Store That Handles Everything."[64] The Fishers not only operated a well-stocked general store but also acted as bankers by loaning money during the early years. These latter activities were taken over by the First National Bank, organized in 1890.[65]

Apparently Big Spring received a great deal of business from Texas and Pacific employees, for in 1887 there were sixteen merchants in the county while the population was only 874.[66] Although the population of Howard County grew rapidly, compared to other sections of West Texas during this period, the optimism of these first businessmen was to an extent misplaced. Of the sixteen merchants in 1887, only eight were still in business by 1890, but five years later the number of mercantile establishments had risen to twelve.[67] At that time the population of the county was estimated at 2,600 and that of Big Spring at 1,200.[68]

[62] U.S., Congress, Senate, Sen. Doc. 64, 31st Cong., 1st sess., 1851, p. 642. The spring flowing from the underlying limestone cap was also used by Comanche Indians as a base for their raids into Mexico (Article in Howard County File, Bureau of Business Research, University of Texas, Austin, Texas).

[63] Louis J. Wortham, *A History of Texas*, V, 307; and Hutto, *Howard County*, no page.

[64] Hutto, *Howard County*, no page; and Shine Philips, *Big Spring, The Casual Biography of a Prairie Town*, p. 130.

[65] Tax Assessor's Roll for Howard County, 1890, Texas, State Archives, Records Division, Austin, Texas.

[66] *First Annual Report of the Agricultural Bureau*, p. 51.

[67] *Fourth Annual Report of the Agricultural Bureau*, p. 140; and *Ninth Annual Report of the Agricultural Bureau*, p. 137.

[68] *Ninth Annual Report of the Agricultural Bureau*, p. 137.

The first school in Howard County was provided for when the Commissioner's Court appropriated $500.00 for the construction of a two-story school building in November 1882. The court also stipulated that the upper room of the structure was to be used as a courtroom six months of the year. The Howard County Common School District was created in 1884, and at that time there were two teachers in the ungraded school.[69] This was the only educational facility in the county until 1891 when two additional schools were built, but by 1895 eight schools with a staff of thirteen teachers were in existence.[70]

There was little improved land in Howard County in the late eighties, and in 1888 there were only two farms in the county. At that time unimproved land was selling for $2.00 to $4.00 an acre, and in 1895 this figure remained unchanged while improved land sold for only $3.00 to $6.00 an acre.[71] Little of the county's land was mortgaged except during years of drought, and the average debt per acre in 1889 was only $1.00.[72] During these years ranching was the principal occupation.

Property evaluation in the county remained fairly steady after rising from $59,184 in 1882 to $1,333,034 in 1884, and by 1895 it stood at $1,178,400.[73] There were few attempts to establish industries of any sort although the 1890 census reported two manufacturing establishments in the county. Public expenditures during this fifteen-year period were also limited, and the citizens of Howard County paid a tax rate that averaged about $.50 per $100.00, and in 1895 the bonded indebtedness was $17,319.[74]

With the exception of Big Spring, the county's trading center, there was no settlement in Howard County by 1895. A few merchants and professional men lived in the county, but the majority of the

[69] *Big Spring* (Texas) *Herald*, April 6, 1938.

[70] *Ninth Annual Report of the Agricultural Bureau*, p. 137.

[71] *Ibid.*; and *Second Annual Report of the Agricultural Bureau*, p. 124.

[72] *Eleventh Census of the United States, 1890: Report of Real Estate Mortgages*, pp. 150, 664.

[73] Tax Assessor's Roll for Howard County, 1882–1895, Texas, State Archives, Records Division, Austin, Texas.

[74] *Ninth Annual Report of the Agricultural Bureau*, p. 137.

residents were engaged in farming and ranching, and the county's wealth was almost completely tied up in land and cattle.

Little development took place in the region south and west of Howard County before 1895. Of the two westernmost counties to be considered, Ector and Midland, the latter was the first organized, and its county seat, the town of Midland, was the first settlement in the area. This town was for years a natural overnight stopping place for travelers between Fort Worth and El Paso since it was halfway between those two cities. In the early eighties when cowboys rode in to pick up mail sacks from passing trains, the town was called Midway because of its location.[75] When the Texas and Pacific ran a line through Midland in 1881, a boxcar was set off and served as post office, depot, and trading house for several years. There was no water supply in the town, and water was hauled in tank cars from Monahans, a distance of about 250 miles, and was emptied into barrels.[76]

The state of Texas and the Texas and Pacific Railroad owned all the land in Midland County in 1881, and the first privately owned ranch, the Chicago Ranch, was established on land purchased from the state by Nelson Morris of Chicago in the early eighties.[77] Other early settlers were the Scharbauers, who had a sheep ranch in the county, and Arthur Johnson, who came to Midland in 1887 and took charge of the JTF Ranch.[78]

In 1891 Nelson Morris offered to pay all local expenses for a government experimental expedition that attempted to make rain on the Chicago Ranch. After a number of trial tests, a major effort to bring rain from cloud formations was made on August 24, 1891. Sticks of dynamite were sent aloft in balloons and exploded, and some 60 mortars, improvised from six-inch well tubing, were fired at the clouds.[79] The test was inconclusive, for although showers fell on the twenty-fifth and twenty-sixth, skeptics pointed out that they had

[75] *El Paso* (Texas) *Times,* July 25, 1948.

[76] Jo Dean Downing, comp., "The Story of Midland," Bureau of Business Research, University of Texas, Austin, Texas, Midland County File.

[77] *Ibid.*

[78] *Midland* (Texas) *Reporter Telegram,* February 29, 1948.

[79] U.S., Congress, Senate, Sen. Doc. 45, 52nd Cong., 1st sess., 1891, pp. 1–21.

been predicted by the United States Weather Bureau in a general forecast for that area.

Local land speculators in Midland did not feel that there was any need for artificial rainmaking. Five years before the experiment on the Chicago Ranch, the Midland Townsite Company employed J. C. Rathburn, publisher of the town's first newspaper, to print 50,000 copies of a pamphlet entitled "Garden of the Southwest, Midland County on the Staked Plains of West Texas, The Most Desirable Locality on the Continent for Homeseekers."[80] The propaganda was at least partially successful, for the population of Midland County rose from 556 in 1887 to 1,033 three years later, and in 1895 it was estimated that 2,000 people lived in the county.[81] A number of small villages made a feeble beginning before 1890, but they either failed completely and passed out of existence or never developed into large towns. By 1890 the town of Midland had a population of 722.[82]

Although the population of the county remained small during this period, business developed at a fairly rapid rate. There were six merchants in the county in 1887 and sixteen by 1895.[83] A private bank with capital of $24,000 and a weekly newspaper had been started in 1888, and two years later a national bank with capital of $60,000 was chartered.[84]

Mortgage debt in Midland County reached a peak in 1884 and then declined until it was almost nonexistent by 1889; however, although the total was small, the average debt per acre was $2.82 during the period from 1880 to 1889 because of the limited number of private holdings in the county.[85] Property evaluations changed little from

---

[80] *Midland Reporter Telegram*, February 29, 1948.

[81] *First Annual Report of the Agricultural Bureau*, p. 52; *Eleventh Census of the United States, 1890: Population*, I, 510; and *Ninth Annual Report of the Agricultural Bureau*, p. 186.

[82] *Eleventh Census of the United States, 1890: Population*, I, 510.

[83] *First Annual Report of the Agricultural Bureau*, p. 52; and *Ninth Annual Report of the Agricultural Bureau*, pp. 186–187.

[84] Tax Assessor's Roll for Midland County, 1888 and 1890, Texas, State Archives, Records Division, Austin, Texas.

[85] *Eleventh Census of the United States, 1890: Report on Real Estate Mortgages*, pp. 150, 670.

the time of county organization until 1895, being $1,061,213 in 1886 and only $100,000 greater in 1895.[86]

Land values were extremely stable since there was little demand at this time. Land sold for $2.00 to $3.00 an acre in 1887, and in 1895 the price was still the same for unimproved land and was $3.00 to $6.00 an acre if improved.[87] The county tax rate was $.625 per $100.00 in 1895, and the county had no indebtedness.[88] By this date the county was still relatively unsettled, and Midland was the only town of any size.

Immediately west of Midland County lay Ector County, until 1891 attached to its eastern neighbor for judicial purposes. There was no settlement in the county until the arrival of the Texas and Pacific. The Texas Railroad Commission required that a section house be built every ten miles along the route of the road, and a boxcar was generally set off to serve this purpose.[89] Small villages, such as Judkins, Badger, and Odessa, began to form around some of these section houses. Because of the lack of water all of them failed except Odessa, where a well was dug by the railroad crew. A store was opened by W. P. Mudgett to serve the needs of the section hands, but there was no building in the settlement until about 1886.[90]

In February 1886 the Texas and Pacific Railroad sold 22 sections of land to John Hoge of Ohio for $53,760.[91] Hoge, a representative of the Townsite Company, subdivided the acreage and sold it in lots for $56.00 each. In 1886 the company published a pamphlet praising Odessa and by 1890 was able to attract ten families from Pennsylvania to the small town.[92] These Pennsylvanians were a group of

[86] Tax Assessor's Roll for Midland County, 1886–1895, Texas, State Archives, Records Division, Austin, Texas.

[87] *First Annual Report of the Agricultural Bureau*, p. 52; and *Ninth Annual Report of the Agricultural Bureau*, pp. 186–187.

[88] *Ninth Annual Report of the Agricultural Bureau*, pp. 186–187.

[89] Finas Wade Horton, "A History of Ector County, Texas" (Master's Thesis, University of Texas, 1950), pp. 54–55.

[90] *Ibid.*, p. 39.

[91] *Ibid.*, p. 39.

[92] *Ibid.*, p. 40.

Methodists who desired to establish a Utopian settlement on the plains of Texas, and they obtained aid from the Townsite Company for their project.[93]

In 1887 the population of Ector County was 126, and two years later the business section of Odessa comprised Mudgett's General Store, a second store built by Nobles and Wyatt, and a hotel operated by R. W. Rathburn consisting of a small lobby, a kitchen, and two sleeping rooms.[94] In 1889 the Townsite Company also erected a building to be used as a college and gave it to the Pennsylvania Methodists to administer.[95] Although the building was never used for its intended purpose, school was held in it for a number of years. The Pennsylvanians also operated a sanitarium in the Odessa community for a short time.

The first school in the county was established in 1890 when J. W. Amburgey instructed 28 private pupils in his home.[96] The same year an attempt was made to form a public school, and Miss Inez Rathburn was paid $57.00 by Midland County for teaching two months at Odessa. In 1891 a permanent public school was founded when Mrs. E. E. Byran conducted classes for seven and one-half months.[97]

The population of the county in 1890 was only 224 and was not growing rapidly. Not much property was owned by individuals; consequently, tax evaluations were low, reaching only $717,052 by 1895.[98] The small population also accounted for the relatively high tax rate of $1.24 per $100.00 on a total indebtedness of $3,596 in

---

[93] The deed from Hoge stated "This lot being sold with the further consideration that it shall never be used for the manufacture or sale of spiritous liquors, malt liquors, or any intoxicating beverages whatever" (Velma Barrett and Hazel Oliver, *Odessa: City of Dreams, A Miracle of the Texas Prairies*, pp. 16–17).

[94] Horton, "History of Ector County," p. 84.

[95] Barrett and Oliver, *Odessa*, p. 5.

[96] Bureau of Business Research, University of Texas, *An Economic Survey of Ector County*, 1.01201.

[97] Horton, "History of Ector County," p. 109.

[98] *Eleventh Census of the United States, 1890: Population,* I, 508; and Tax Assessor's Roll for Ector County, 1895, Texas, State Archives, Records Division, Austin, Texas.

1891; however, by 1895 the tax rate had been lowered to $.67 per $100.00.[99]

Stock raising remained the principal, indeed, almost the only, occupation of the people of Ector County during its first years of existence, and by the late nineties Odessa was an important cattle shipping point. Wealth was entirely in land and cattle, and the land was valued at $2.00 to $5.00 if improved, and $1.00 to $3.00 if unimproved.[100] There was almost no improved land in the county, nor did the amount increase greatly because more acreage was devoted to cattle raising as ranchers moved west.

Dawson County, north and east of Ector County, was the last of the counties under consideration to be organized. The county was originally the property of John Cameron, who received it as a Mexican land grant.[101] Ranching was established early, and in 1854 Lamesa, the county seat, was laid out by Frank Connor, a cowboy from a nearby ranch, and a surveyor, C. C. Coty Jr.[102] By 1860 there were 281 people living in Dawson County, but apparently they all left during the Civil War, for there was no population recorded in 1870.[103]

A few people began to drift in during the eighteen-seventies, but the county population did not reach 100 until after the turn of the century.[104] Attached to Howard County until its organization in 1905, Dawson County was throughout this period an almost unsettled ranching area. There was neither transportation nor water to encourage people to push so far west, and not until after its organization did the county receive any amount of immigration.

Between the time the first settlers arrived in West Texas in the

[99] *Fifth Annual Report of the Agricultural Bureau*, p. 88; and *Ninth Annual Report of the Agricultural Bureau*, p. 85.

[100] *Fifth Annual Report of the Agricultural Bureau*, p. 88.

[101] Raymond F. Neill, *History of Dawson County*, p. 4.

[102] *Ibid.*; and Bureau of Business Research, University of Texas, *An Economic Survey of Dawson County*, 1.03.

[103] Texas, Department of Agriculture, *Year Book, 1909*, p. 115.

[104] *Ibid.*; and Bureau of Business Research, University of Texas, *An Economic Survey of Dawson County*, 1.03.

late seventies and 1895, the counties in the area between the thirty-first and thirty-third parallels underwent a great development. During this period the first pioneers moved across the one-hundredth meridian into West Texas, the cattle industry of the open range reached a peak of development and was in turn supplanted by fenced ranches that finally gave way to farming, and the early settlements were growing into permanent towns. Although the presence of the Texas and Pacific Railroad in some of the counties gave assurance that the towns would probably continue in existence, there were few indications in the late nineties that West Texas would ever be anything other than an economically poor farming and ranching area. In 1895 residents were still trying to grub an existence on the West Texas soil either by farming or by raising cattle. In both cases they were to a large degree dependent upon the whims of the weather and the markets. Merchants in the few scattered towns were in turn dependent upon these settlers for their business.

Life in West Texas in the nineties was a drab affair, rarely relieved by any excitement. This perhaps accounted for the large percentage of church members in the area, for at church meetings the residents could find some change from their everyday life.[105] They also took an active interest in state and national political contests, always casting their lots with the Democratic Party by an overwhelming majority.[106] Economically the area was still dependent on ranching in 1895.[107] The few attempts at manufacturing had, for the most part,

[105] Total church membership of all denominations in 1890 was: Midland County, 241; Howard County, 269; Ector County, 51; Nolan County, 411; and Scurry County, 600 (*Eleventh Census of the United States, 1890: Report of Church Statistics*, pp. 83, 166, 187, 246, 352, 571, 589, 687, 717.

[106] In the Texas Gubernatorial election of 1890 over 1,400 votes were cast for the Democratic candidate as opposed to less than 200 for the Republican nominee (*Fourth Annual Report of the Agricultural Bureau*, pp. 140, 185, 201, and 256). In the Presidential election of 1896 the vote was 1,068 Democratic to 228 Republican (*Ninth Annual Report of the Agricultural Bureau*, p. 415).

[107] The total number of cattle in the six counties in 1895 was approximately 90,000, the number of sheep about 30,000, and the total value of livestock was nearly $900,000 (*Ninth Annual Report of the Agricultural Bureau*, pp. 137–201).

been total failures. Farming had been started, but the farmers were yet to prove that the region could support extensive crop production, and the problems confronting farmers in the semiarid section were many and complex.

CHAPTER THREE

THE DEVELOPMENT OF AGRICULTURE, 1880–1900

ALTHOUGH THE MOST IMPORTANT early industry in central West Texas was cattle raising, a majority of the settlers engaged in farming to some extent. Immigration and land companies, in attempts to bring as many people as possible into the area, encouraged prospective farmers by pointing out the adaptability of the area to crop raising. Settlers were told that although ranching returned large profits, it also required a great deal of capital investment, whereas farming could be begun with little ready cash. Consequently, attempts were made to raise crops almost from the time the first pioneers moved into the area.

As in other parts of the Great Plains, the West Texas climate and soil presented a number of serious problems to farmers coming from other regions. Moving from areas where a fairly abundant supply of water and timber was available, settlers advancing west of the one-hundredth meridian found that they had to adapt themselves and their farming methods to new conditions. Probably the most serious, and certainly the most immediate, problem to be solved was that of providing an adequate water supply.

The average annual rainfall in Texas decreased progressively from east to west, and nearly all West Texas lay in a semiarid part of the state. In the eastern section of this region the average rainfall in Scurry County over a twenty-eight–year period beginning in 1888 was 22.60 inches, the average in Howard County over thirty-eight years after 1891 was 18.70 inches annually, and in the far western section, Midland and Ector counties, the average during thirty-one years for which reports were complete after 1885 was 16.35 inches a year.[1]

Not only was the amount of rainfall limited, but there were also years of extreme drought during which there was little or no precipitation to record. In 1917 rainfall in West Texas was almost non-existent, and the area suffered from a drought, the effects of which were second only to the dry years of the mid-eighties. Precipitation in 1917 measured only 5.52 inches in Ector County and 4.80 inches in Howard County.[2] Moreover, rain, when it occurred, was often torrential, so that a great deal of the moisture was lost by runoff, and it fell only locally, bringing little general relief. As a result the farmer could seldom rely on a regular supply of water in the form of rainfall.

In addition to these difficulties, during the summer months the prevailing wind in West Texas was from the south, and the rate of evaporation was extremely high in most of the area. Only one bright spot existed in this otherwise gloomy picture of the water problem in West Texas: about 80 per cent of the precipitation fell in the seven months from April to October, and during this period rain fell at fairly regular intervals.[3] The farmer might therefore hope for some rainfall during a large part of the growing season.

Since it was known that precipitation was limited, many immigration brochures misled prospective settlers into believing that water was easily obtainable by drilling wells. In 1874 the Southwestern Immigration Company assured farmers that since sufficient rainfall could not be anticipated in most of West Texas, "At other points it will be necessary to construct ponds or tanks, and to dig bore wells. About half way across the staked plains water is found by digging a

[1] Penn Livingston and Robert R. Bennett, *Geology and Ground Water Resources of the Big Spring Area, Texas*, pp. 7–8; and D. B. Knowles, *Ground-Water Resources of Ector County, Texas*, pp. 4–5.

[2] Livingston and Bennett, *Geology and Ground Water Resources*, pp. 7–8.

[3] *Ibid.*

few feet."[4] The popular misconception that water lay only a few feet beneath the surface of the ground was thus planted in the minds of many people. Willing believers were to be disappointed, for, although a large ground-water supply existed in West Texas, it was to be found at depths usually in excess of 100 feet. Ground water was eventually to be the solution to the water problem in this area; however, it was not until the windmill was introduced in large numbers after 1890 that wells furnished an adequate water supply. Even then bored wells were of limited use to the farmer because he usually was able to obtain only enough water for household use and for watering a few cattle. Not until the appearance of powerful pumps, mostly after 1940, were wells utilized to any extent for irrigation purposes.

A second difficulty to be overcome by immigrants to the area between the one-hundredth meridian and the New Mexico border was the lack of wood. Since most of West Texas had at best a few stunted oak, cedar, or mesquite trees, lumber for homes had to be imported. The first settlers in the region solved the problem by living in tents or dugouts until lumber became available.[5] Fortunately for these pioneers, the railroad reached West Texas in 1881, and lumber was among the first freight shipped to the small settlements.

Finding material for fencing never posed a serious problem for the farmer since he generally opposed fencing during the seventies and eighties when barbed wire was first introduced into the area. This opposition was created when overzealous ranchers made such extensive use of barbed wire that it was not uncommon for farmers to find their small holdings completely surrounded by the fences of cattlemen. As a result, West Texas farmers never did fence to any extent, but the few who did used barbed wire, the only practical material in the section.

The scarcity of wood was never a serious obstacle to those with money to purchase lumber because the railroad provided a supply of

[4] Millicent Seay Huff, "A Study of Work Done by Texas Railroad Companies to Encourage Immigration into Texas between 1870 and 1890" (Master's Thesis, University of Texas, 1955), p. 34.

[5] Kathryn Cotten, *Saga of Scurry*, p. 6; and Louise Bradford, "A History of Nolan County Texas" (Master's Thesis, University of Texas, 1934), p. 66.

building materials almost from the time the first settlers arrived on the scene. It was the lack of water and the necessity of discovering farming methods suitable to a semiarid region that caused the greatest difficulty for farmers. Despite the troubles encountered, immigrants began raising crops during the eighties, although farming was not economically important until a few years later.

Crop production was first reported in the area under consideration in 1880, when 856 acres were tilled in Nolan County, the scene of the earliest agricultural development; 330 bushels of Indian corn were produced on 64 acres.[6] The following year Nolan County became the first county in the area in which cotton was raised; a farmer named Fisher hauled cotton to Abilene, Taylor County, where he had it ginned.[7]

By 1895 the *Taylor County News* was predicting a bright future for agriculture in West Texas when it reported that "one of the most profitable crops that can be raised in this country is broomcorn," and with considerable insight stated that "there is nothing a farmer can plant that will pay him better than sorghum which will make three crops a year."[8] The production of sorghum was eventually to become one of the mainstays of West Texas farms.

The following year, 1886, the *News* claimed that the adaptability of West Texas soil to farming was a proven fact, that the period of experimentation was past, and that almost all crops "grow to perfection here."[9] Proof of variety in crop production was given by citing the example of G. R. West who had raised 30 bushels of wheat per acre in 1885.

The optimistic attitude of the *News* was not substantiated by fact, for in the late eighties farming was still in its infancy, and there was

[6] U.S., Department of Commerce, Bureau of the Census, *Tenth Census of the United States, 1880: Agriculture*, pp. 664–668.

[7] Bradford, "History of Nolan County," p. 41.

[8] *Taylor County* (Texas) *News*, April 3, 1885.

[9] *Ibid.*, March 5, 1886. Apparently the estimates of the future of farming in the area made by the editor depended a great deal on the situation at the moment, for in 1885 the paper said that "The idea that this part of Texas will ever be an agricultural country is a great joke of huge proportions" (*ibid.*, June 1, 1885).

some question as to whether or not it would ever become an important factor in the West Texas economy. The drought of 1886–1887 was a severe setback to farming in the area with damage to all crops ranging from an estimated 85 per cent in Scurry County to 93 per cent in Nolan County, these losses being typical of the entire region.[10] As a result, the only farm product reported in the Texas *First Annual Report of the Agricultural Bureau* (1887) was wool. In the six counties under consideration, excluding Ector and Dawson counties, which had no production, a total of 775,968 pounds of wool valued at $100,867 was clipped from 120,861 sheep.[11]

By 1888 farmers who had outlasted the drought and had remained in Nolan County were again able to make crops, and in that year a variety of production was reported, including 44 bales of cotton, 8,370 bushels of corn, 2,900 bushels of wheat, 27,500 bushels of oats, and 915 tons of sorghum.[12] The next year there were 87 farms in the county employing eight farm laborers whose pay averaged $20.00 a month.[13] Production of most crops was about the same as in 1888 although the amount of cotton had increased to 72 bales, and that of sorghum to 1,639 tons.[14] By the 1890 census the number of farms in Nolan County had nearly doubled. Of the 169 farms in the county at that time, 139 were operated by owners, and very little tenancy existed; 2 farms were rented for money and 2 were farmed on shares.[15] Of the 85,196 acres in farms, 54,387 were improved, and an estimated $47,020 worth of farm products was raised.[16] Nearly all the farm production was consumed on the farms.

[10] Texas, Department of Agriculture, *First Annual Report of the Agricultural Bureau of the Department of Agriculture, Insurance, Statistics, and History,* pp. 169, 200.

[11] *Ibid.,* pp. 109, 158, 169, 200.

[12] *Second Annual Report of the Agricultural Bureau,* p. 191.

[13] *Third Annual Report of the Agricultural Bureau,* p. 188.

[14] Corn production was 15,288 bushels, wheat 5,800 bushels, and oats 24,970 (*ibid.*).

[15] *Eleventh Census of the United States, 1890: Report of Statistics of Agriculture,* pp. 186–187. In a few cases the figures given by the United States Census and those of state agencies conflict. Unless some other determining factor was available, the federal figures were used.

[16] Production of specific crops and acreage of each was: 566 bushels of

From a financial point of view ranching was still the major industry in 1890. The wool clip of 1889–1890 in Nolan County was
reported as 195,792 pounds from 38,350 sheep.[17] The number of
cattle in 1890 was 23,875 valued at more than $250,000.[18] Thus,
profits from ranching far surpassed those from crop raising.

Until 1890 there was little development in farming, but in the
decade from 1890 to 1900 farming made substantial gains in Nolan
County. By the end of this period there were 293 farms in the
county.[19] Tenancy was increasing slowly throughout the period but
had not reached serious proportions. Only 5 farms were rented in
1893, but by 1900 there were 6 cash tenants and 36 share tenants.[20]
The use of farm labor was also becoming more common, and as
early as 1893, 50 farm workers were employed at salaries averaging
$13.00 a month.[21] Improved farm and ranch acreage rose to 179,640
acres of a total of 390,372 by 1900, land and improvements being
valued at $890,480.[22]

Although crop production rose very slowly during the decade,
farming had become a permanent, though not yet an economically
important, part of the scene by 1895. Production of the principal
crops in that year included 299 bales of cotton, 19,419 bushels of
oats, 1,954 tons of sorghum, 12,022 bushels of corn, and 6,722
bushels of wheat.[23] With the single exception of wheat, crop production rose significantly during the next five years. In 1900 Nolan
County farmers reported 1,830 bales of cotton, 56,100 bushels of
corn, 21,010 bushels of oats, 4,198 tons of forage crops, and 4,490
bushels of wheat.[24] Dairy products, although of little commercial

barley on 29 acres; 14,183 bushels of corn on 563 acres; 26,142 bushels of oats
on 900 acres; 1,023 bushels of rye on 80 acres, and 6,399 bushels of wheat on
448 acres (*ibid.*, pp. 186–187).

[17] *Ibid.*, pp. 186–187.
[18] *Ibid.*, pp. 230, 387.
[19] *Twelfth Census of the United States, 1900: Agriculture*, I, 128.
[20] *Ibid.*; and *Seventh Annual Report of the Agricultural Bureau*, p. 370.
[21] *Seventh Annual Report of the Agricultural Bureau*, p. 370.
[22] *Twelfth Census of the United States, 1900: Agriculture*, I, 300.
[23] *Ninth Annual Report of the Agricultural Bureau*, p. 237.
[24] *Twelfth Census of the United States, 1900: Agriculture*, II, 186, 485, 262.

importance since most of them were consumed on the farms, were valued at $10,660 in 1899.[25]

Despite gains made in crop production throughout the decade, ranching continued to dominate the agricultural scene. The total number of cattle and sheep reached a peak in 1891 when there were 23,437 cattle and 11,113 sheep in Nolan County.[26] The number of livestock declined slightly thereafter until 1900 when the number of cattle rose to a total of 23,998 valued at $276,388.[27] Receipts from the sale of livestock totaled $54,392 in 1899, but wool production in that year was only 20,500 pounds, a considerable drop from the amount in 1890 due to the decreasing number of sheep in the county.[28]

In Scurry County farming was just beginning in the late eighties. In 1888 there were 48 farms in the county with a total production of 1,800 bushels of corn, 40 bushels of wheat, 3,210 bushels of oats, and 1,366 tons of sorghum.[29] Apparently the experiences of farmers in 1888 encouraged other residents to plant crops, for the following year 114 farms were operated in the county. Three farms were rented, and seventeen farm laborers were employed at average wages of $20.00 a month. In addition to slightly larger yields of all crops over the previous year, the first cotton, eighteen bales, was ginned in 1889.[30]

The constant movement of people into the area and the success of those engaged in farming continued to attract more people to the occupation; by 1890, 184 farms were operated in the county,[31] although that number had declined to 158 in 1895. Of these, 43 were rented for money, and one was worked on shares. Farm products

[25] *Ibid.*, I, 623.

[26] *Fifth Annual Report of the Agricultural Bureau*, p. 239.

[27] Texas, Department of Agriculture, *Year Book, 1909*, p. 164.

[28] *Twelfth Census of the United States, 1900: Agriculture*, I, 623.

[29] *Second Annual Report of the Agricultural Bureau*, p. 221. The average size of farms at this time was about 700 acres. Farms were large because most farmers also grazed livestock.

[30] *Third Annual Report of the Agricultural Bureau*, p. 224.

[31] *Eleventh Census of the United States, 1890: Report of Statistics of Agriculture*, pp. 186–187.

were valued at an estimated $60,270 in 1890. Scurry County farmers cultivated 124,158 acres, but they were doing little to improve production other than trusting to the whims of the weather, for in that year only $6.00 was spent on fertilizer.[32]

Throughout the early years farming remained a relatively simple process in these counties. Typical of the area was Scurry County where few farm laborers were hired during the 1890–1895 period. There were 23 workers on farms in 1890 when their average wages were $12.56 a month, and five years later the number had declined to 12 laborers whose pay averaged $16.66 a month.[33] Most farms were operated by the farmer and his family without any hired hands, and tenancy was relatively unimportant.[34] Nor did West Texas farmers make any extensive use of machinery in connection with raising crops prior to 1895. The total value of farm implements in 1890 was $4,857 in Scurry County, an average of about $26.00 per farm, and two years later the total investment was only $3,160.[35] Farm production rose slowly, the principal crops being corn, maize, and sorghum. Wheat was fast becoming an important field crop, and over 7,000 bushels were raised in 1893.[36] Cotton was apparently grown on a very limited basis, for in 1895 only 401 bales were ginned, a decrease of 79 bales from 1890.[37]

Tenancy made some inroads by the turn of the century, for in 1900 there were 5 renters and 28 sharecroppers on the 586 farms and ranches in the county.[38] Most land was utilized by ranchers, for of the 702,776 acres devoted to agriculture, less than 35,000

[32] *Ibid.*, p. 230.

[33] *Fourth Annual Report of the Agricultural Bureau*, p. 256; and *Ninth Annual Report of the Agricultural Bureau*, p. 231.

[34] *Fourth* through *Ninth Annual Report of the Agricultural Bureau*. These reports cover the period from 1890 to 1895.

[35] *Fourth Annual Report of the Agricultural Bureau*, p. 256; and *Sixth Annual Report of the Agricultural Bureau*, p. 293.

[36] *Seventh Annual Report of the Agricultural Bureau*, p. 231.

[37] *Eleventh Census of the United States, 1890: Report of Statistics of Agriculture*, p. 397; and *Ninth Annual Report of the Agricultural Bureau*, p. 237.

[38] *Twelfth Census of the United States, 1900: Agriculture*, I, 130.

acres were improved.[39] Further evidence of the dominance of ranching was the fact that $162,728 was received from the sale of livestock in 1899.[40] Moreover, there were 23,823 cattle in Scurry County valued at $300,954 in 1900. Sheep were also raised in the county, and the 1899–1900 wool clip was 13,790 pounds.[41]

Although ranching continued to be more important than farming, crop production was constantly increasing. Cotton production had made an appreciable rise by 1900. Only 900 bales of cotton were ginned in 1899, but the following year farmers reported raising 2,860 bales on 7,422 acres.[42] Yields of other crops had risen also, corn providing the largest production with 75,680 bushels, and wheat and oats being considerably less, 6,220 bushels and 7,240 bushels respectively.[43] Forage crops made 8,530 tons, 5,057 tons of millet was harvested, and in addition to crops, Scurry County farmers produced $26,630 worth of dairy products.[44]

Agriculture in Scurry County, as in all of the area under consideration, was a definite, although still a secondary, factor in the economy of the county. Most of the farm production was consumed in the county, a great deal of it on the farms, and consequently little cash profit was realized by the individual farmer. However, farmers had demonstrated that crops could be raised in large quantities, thus providing a basis for future expansion into commercial production.

Other West Texas counties witnessed a somewhat similar agricultural development between 1890 and 1900. In Howard County the first crops were not reported until 1889 when there were two farms in the county.[45] Various crops were grown on a limited basis,

---

[39] *Ibid.*, p. 301.

[40] *Twelfth Census of the United States, 1900: Agriculture*, I, 484–485.

[41] *Ibid.*, p. 682; and Texas, Department of Agriculture, *Year Book, 1909*, p. 172.

[42] *Twelfth Census of the United States, 1900: Agriculture*, I, 485.

[43] *Ibid.*, p. 186.

[44] *Ibid.*, p. 623; and Texas, Department of Agriculture, *Year Book, 1909*, p. 170.

[45] *Third Annual Report of the Agricultural Bureau*, p. 120.

the principal yield being 500 bushels of corn from 28 acres.[46] Farm production in 1890 fell below that of the previous year, and it was not until 1891 that Howard County farming demonstrated any signs of being a permanent part of the agricultural scene.

Of the 31 farms in the county in 1891 only 2 were rented, and farmers employed 6 laborers at an average wage of $25.00 a month. Total reported crops included 32 bales of cotton and 215 tons of sorghum as livestock remained the chief source of agricultural revenue. At the time ranchers grazed 15,820 cattle valued at $105,034 and 13,925 sheep worth $20,448; the 34,560-pound wool clip in 1891 was estimated at $3,970.[47]

The number of farms in Howard County varied considerably from year to year—a result of the uncertainty involved in establishing a new industry and the lack of adequate markets. There were 83 farms in 1892, 60 the following year, only 18 in 1895, and 130 at the end of the decade.[48] Only one person rented a farm in 1895, but five years later 7 cash tenants and 13 share tenants cultivated land in the county.[49] Laborers were used throughout the decade, usually only during cotton-picking season, the largest number being 60 in 1893 and decreasing to 10 by 1895.[50] In 1900, $14,460 was spent on farm labor, so it was still of minor importance since wages averaged only $20.00 a month.[51] A fairly large amount of money was invested in farm implements considering how few farms existed; the amount rose from $1,110 in 1893 to $1,255 two years later.[52]

[46] Other crops produced were 2 bales of cotton on 4 acres; 70 tons of hay on 120 acres; 50 bushels of wheat on 6 acres; and 184 tons of sorghum (*ibid.*).

[47] *Fifth Annual Report of the Agricultural Bureau*, p. 155.

[48] *Sixth Annual Report of the Agricultural Bureau*, p. 165; *Seventh Annual Report of the Agricultural Bureau*, p. 241; *Ninth Annual Report of the Agricultural Bureau*, p. 137; and *Twelfth Census of the United States, 1900: Agriculture*, I, 126.

[49] *Ninth Annual Report of the Agricultural Bureau*, p. 137; and *Twelfth Census of the United States, 1900: Agriculture*, I, 126.

[50] *Seventh Annual Report of the Agricultural Bureau*, p. 241; and *Ninth Annual Report of the Agricultural Bureau*, p. 137.

[51] *Twelfth Census of the United States, 1900: Agriculture*, I, 300.

[52] *Seventh Annual Report of the Agricultural Bureau*, p. 241; and *Ninth Annual Report of the Agricultural Bureau*, p. 137.

Improved acreage in Howard County varied as did the number of farms. In 1893 there were 1,678 acres under cultivation, and in 1900 crops were raised on 5,835 acres. The principal crops throughout this period were corn and sorghum, which made 1,814 bushels and 2,353 tons respectively in 1893 and 4,450 bushels and 1,503 tons in 1900.[53] Attempts were made to grow other crops, and for one year only, 1893, a production of 1,215 tons of molasses cane was reported.[54] Success in raising cotton was limited, but farmers continued to plant the crop, and production rose gradually from 31 bales in 1895 to 199 bales five years later.[55] Dairy products on Howard County farms were also of some value, and in 1899 such produce was worth $10,660.[56]

Some ranchers in the county were encouraging farming as late as 1900 because crop raising in the area had proven increasingly successful. Cotton, corn, maize, oats, and wheat were planted on the Lucien Wells Ranch near Big Spring in 1900, but the only production reported was two bales of cotton on three acres.[57]

Despite the encouragement by some ranchers, the small gains made in crop farming were little challenge to the position of ranching as the most important industry at the turn of the century. Stock raising, with emphasis almost exclusively on cattle, dominated the economy of Howard County. In 1899, $92,517 was received from the sale of livestock, all from cattle since there were few sheep in the county.[58] The 21,928 cattle in Howard County in 1900 were valued at $265,960.[59]

West of Howard County there was little farming before 1900, and livestock raising was almost the sole occupation of residents in the

[53] *Seventh Annual Report of the Agricultural Bureau*, p. 241; and *Twelfth Census of the United States, 1900: Agriculture*, I, 300.

[54] *Seventh Annual Report of the Agricultural Bureau*, p. 241.

[55] *Ninth Annual Report of the Agricultural Bureau*, p. 137; and *Twelfth Census of the United States, 1900: Agriculture*, II, 484.

[56] *Twelfth Census of the United States, 1900: Agriculture*, I, 622.

[57] John Allison Rickard, "The Ranch Industry of the Texas South Plains" (Master's Thesis, University of Texas, 1927), pp. 165–166.

[58] *Twelfth Census of the United States, 1900: Agriculture*, I, 482–483, 682.

[59] Texas, Department of Agriculture, *Year Book, 1909*, p. 149.

far western part of the state. In Midland County farmers attempted to raise crops until about 1893, when most of the experiments were given up as failures; not until 1900 was production again reported. At the start of the decade there were 29 farms in the county, all cultivated by the owners. Only 147 acres of land were improved, and the estimated value of all farm products was barely over $7,000.[60] In 1892 the only crop reported was 15 tons of sorghum, and during the rest of the nineties there was no agricultural production at all.[61] In 1900 a few individuals were still trying to farm, and 30 bushels of oats, 20 bushels of rye, and 270 tons of forage crops were reported grown on 897 acres.[62] In addition to crops, $5,337 worth of dairy products on 57 farms was reported.[63]

Livestock was the principal source of income in Midland County during this period. The 1889–1890 wool clip amounted to 114,600 pounds from 13,364 sheep, and there were 29,421 cattle in the county.[64] The total value of livestock in 1891 was estimated at $141,760 in addition to a wool production of 270,000 pounds at $.10 a pound.[65] In 1899, $195,951 was received from the sale of livestock, and 30,500 pounds of wool were clipped.[66] The following year Midland County ranchers grazed 14,096 cattle and 4,000 sheep, valued at $184,727.[67]

A similar situation existed during the nineties in Ector County. Although early attempts to farm were made by Charlie White in 1890 when he planted several acres of sorghum just south of Odessa, the experiment was not commercially successful, for no agricultural

[60] *Eleventh Census of the United States, 1890: Report of Statistics of Agriculture*, p. 186.

[61] *Sixth Annual Report of the Agricultural Bureau*, p. 232. The Bureau showed no crop production after 1892.

[62] *Twelfth Census of the United States, 1900: Agriculture*, II, 186, 262, 874.

[63] *Ibid.*, I, 623.

[64] *Eleventh Census of the United States, 1890: Report of Statistics of Agriculture*, pp. 268, 309.

[65] *Fifth Annual Report of the Agricultural Bureau*, p. 222.

[66] *Twelfth Census of the United States, 1900: Agriculture*, I, 482–483, 682.

[67] Texas, Department of Agriculture, *Year Book, 1909*, p. 161.

production was reported for the county by 1900.[68] In 1895 there were 128 acres in cultivation, and farmers had invested $44.00 in farm implements, but no crops were raised.[69] By 1900 only 92 acres were under cultivation, and there was still no report of crops being produced.[70]

Cattle and sheep raising dominated the agricultural scene in Ector County during the decade. In 1891, 7,000 sheep were sheared, and the 42,000 pounds of wool brought $8,400. At that time there were 11,120 cattle in the county valued at more than $50,000, and about the same number of sheep worth $16,680.[71] The number of livestock remained relatively unchanged through 1895 when the total value was $93,490.[72] By 1900, as more people moved into the county and established ranches, the number of cattle increased. At the end of the decade there were 17,214 cattle in Ector County, and in 1899 $68,468 was realized from the sale of livestock.[73] Profits from agriculture, other than livestock raising, were still a thing of the future in far western Texas in 1900.

Dawson County agriculture was strictly limited to cattle ranching before 1900, and there was very little of that. In 1900 only 37 people, mainly cowboys, lived in the county, and there were five ranches in operation.[74] A total of 9,900 cattle valued at $118,200 were grazed, and there were no sheep.[75] About $30,000 was realized from the sale of livestock in 1899.[76] There was no farming on Dawson County land, and development of that occupation had to await the arrival of more settlers.

Farming in central West Texas during the period before 1900

[68] White also attempted to raise cotton in 1891 with little success (Velma Barrett and Hazel Oliver, *Odessa: City of Dreams, A Miracle of the Texas Prairies*, p. 46).

[69] *Ninth Annual Report of the Agricultural Bureau*, p. 85.

[70] *Twelfth Census of the United States, 1900: Agriculture*, I, 299.

[71] *Fifth Annual Report of the Agricultural Bureau*, p. 88.

[72] *Ninth Annual Report of the Agricultural Bureau*, p. 85.

[73] Texas, Department of Agriculture, *Year Book, 1909*, p. 137; and *Twelfth Census of the United States, 1900: Agriculture*, I, 481.

[74] Texas, Department of Agriculture, *Year Book, 1909*, p. 115.

[75] *Ibid.*, p. 325.

[76] *Twelfth Census of the United States, 1900: Agriculture*, I, 480–481.

could be considered little more than a secondary occupation when related to the economy as a whole. The hazards encountered by farmers were numerous, and they often appeared insurmountable. The lack of rainfall and periods of drought made farming at best an uncertain endeavor. In addition, the difficulty of discovering a successful method of farming in an unfavorable climate presented a problem. Because of this unpromising set of circumstances farming made very little progress during the period. Moreover, it was at a disadvantage when compared to ranching and could not compete on an equal basis for capital and labor resources.

Despite the slow rate of development of the industry, crop raising was on a sound footing in much of the area under consideration by 1900. The most successful crops had been discovered, and acreage and production were increasing. In the counties in which farming had a good beginning, land values were rising, whereas the price of land in counties almost wholly devoted to ranching remained lower.[77] In Nolan and Scurry counties, where farming had become more important, improved land sold for $7.00 to about $20.00 an acre, whereas in Ector County and Midland County land was worth only $2.00 to $6.00 an acre.[78]

Farming had made some progress in the area, but in only three counties, Nolan, Scurry, and Howard, was there any crop production of consequence, and in only one, Nolan County, was farming of real importance by 1900. In Dawson, Midland, and Ector counties farming had hardly begun. The 1,107 farms in the six counties were generally farmed by the owners although 173 were operated by cash or share tenants.[79] Improved land in the area totaled 224,608 acres, a majority of which were in Nolan County.[80]

[77] Total area of land and its value in the six counties was: Nolan County, 551,000 acres at $994,510; Scurry County, 406,617 acres at $521,281; Howard County, 362,462 acres at $368,450; Midland County, 281,811 acres at $300,932; and Ector County, 252,235 acres at $253,084. No figures were given for Dawson County other than that land was about $1.00 an acre (Texas, Department of Agriculture, *Year Book, 1909*, pp. 134, 137, 149, 161, 164, 172).

[78] *Ninth Annual Report of the Agricultural Bureau*, pp. 137, 169, 201.

[79] *Twelfth Census of the United States, 1900: Agriculture*, I, 126–130.

[80] *Ibid.*, pp. 299–301.

The principal crop grown in West Texas at the turn of the century, in terms of cash returns and acreage devoted to cultivation, was cotton, and forage crops held second place. Corn, wheat, and oats were the other important crops.[81] The total estimated value of crops produced in the five counties reporting production in 1900 was a little more than $400,000, and cotton accounted for about one-third of this amount.[82] Besides crops, dairy products from farms in the area were valued at $53,964.[83] In contrast, the value of livestock in 1900 was $1,310,171.[84] Farming in West Texas was definitely in its infancy at the end of the nineteenth century, but the progress made between 1890 and 1900 indicated that the industry would mature rapidly.

[81] Total crop production in 1900 was: 28,280 bushels of oats; 10,760 bushels of wheat; 136,230 bushels of corn; 4,889 bales of cotton; 14,501 tons of forage crops; and 560 bushels of rye (*Twelfth Census of the United States, 1900: Agriculture*, I, 185–186, 262, 484–485). Forage crops were used for feed on the farms.

[82] These estimates were made by using average prices from the U.S., Department of Agriculture, *Yearbook of the United States Department of Agriculture*, 1900.

[83] *Twelfth Census of the United States, 1900: Agriculture*, I, 623.

[84] Texas, Department of Agriculture, *Year Book, 1909*, p. 172.

CHAPTER FOUR

WEST TEXAS AGRICULTURE, 1900–1930

DURING THE FIRST DECADE of the twentieth century the population of the six counties under consideration more than doubled. As a result all aspects of the economic life of the area expanded, especially agriculture, since most of the newcomers became farmers. Although the proceeds from farm production lagged behind those of ranching in 1900, farming became increasingly important during the first years of the decade, and by 1910 had become the more important source of income in at least half of the counties concerned.

Two other factors which affected West Texas farmers during this period were a severe drought in 1903 and the creation of the Texas Department of Agriculture in 1907. In the early summer of 1903, rains ceased to fall on the Texas plains, and the grass began to fail.[1] As a result, cattle prices declined, many breeders abandoned pastures under lease since they were unable to keep up the $.03 per acre lease price, and production of some crops on farms was considerably less than in the previous year.[2] The establishment of a state Department of Agriculture did not immediately influence farming, but in the years following its founding, programs of the department to en-

---

[1] Texas, Commissioner of the General Land Office, *Biennial Report of the Commissioner of the General Land Office of Texas,* 1902–1904, p. 15.

[2] By 1904 the worst part of the drought was over (Texas, Department of Agriculture, *Year Book, 1909,* p. 340).

courage farmers' organizations and the publication of technical bulletins aided farmers in all parts of the state.[3]

Typical of farm groups influenced by the Texas Department of Agriculture were the Farmers Institutes. In 1910 the Commissioner of Agriculture said that he regarded these institutes as second to no other medium for "arousing interest among farmers in scientific agriculture and acquainting them to apply the latest and best methods."[4] Lecturers sent by the organization traveled throughout the state, and in 1916 they addressed 1,595 meetings of the institutes and 1,128 other public gatherings, such as picnics, Farmers Union, and Good Road groups, with a total estimated attendance of 273,000.[5] In addition to lectures on scientific agriculture, demonstrations of farming methods, such as terracing to prevent erosion, were given. Field forces of the organization were also required to make investigations concerning insects, pests, and plant diseases in order to improve farming in the state.

By the spring and summer of 1910 the movement had spread to the western part of the state, and Farmers Institutes were being organized. In May of that year an institute was formed at Big Spring, Howard County, with 84 members.[6] During July and August similar organizational meetings were held at Sweetwater, Nolan County, with a total of 20 farmers present.[7] In the following year Scurry County farmers held their first meeting at Snyder, and in 1912 Midland was added to the list of West Texas counties having Farmers Institutes.[8] Although additional chapters were begun, including one in Ector County, in the years before World War I, the number of meetings gradually decreased, and during the war the organization slowly passed out of existence in West Texas.

The formation of the Farmers Institutes indicated an increased

---

[3] Texas, Department of Agriculture, *Third Annual Report of the Commissioner of Agriculture*, p. 10.

[4] *Ibid.*

[5] *Ninth Annual Report of the Commissioner of Agriculture*, pp. 8–9.

[6] *Third Annual Report of the Commissioner of Agriculture*, pp. 11–13.

[7] Two organizational meetings were needed before a chapter was formed at Sweetwater during the summer of 1910 (*ibid.*).

[8] *Fourth Annual Report of the Commissioner of Agriculture*, p. 11; and *Fifth Annual Report of the Commissioner of Agriculture*, pp. 13–21.

interest in farming in West Texas which was principally the result of
a rapidly growing population in the area. Representative of the area
was Nolan County in which the number of people rose from 2,611 in
1900 to almost 12,000 ten years later.[9] The urban population increased 523.3 per cent during this decade whereas in rural areas
growth only reached 303 per cent. The farm population was greater,
however, since 7,823 people lived outside of towns while fewer than
5,000 lived in urban places.[10]

The increased farm population inevitably resulted in greater crop
production. A variety of crops was grown, including cotton, corn,
oats, kaffir corn, and milo maize, but the rising importance of farming
was best demonstrated by the large production of two staples, cotton
and cereal crops. Nolan County cotton production rose from 2,536
bales in 1900 to 4,882 in 1904, and 10,731 in 1910, and the amount
of cereal crops grown reached 396,694 bushels by 1910.[11] By the
latter date farming had created a demand for other businesses in
the county, and there were a flour mill, a cottonseed-oil mill, and a
number of cotton gins in Sweetwater.[12]

It was during the first decade of the century that the receipts from
farm products first outstripped those from livestock raising. In 1909,
$335,661 was realized from the sale of animals, whereas the total
value of all crops was $795,431.[13] In addition to crops, Nolan County
farmers obtained nearly $25,000 from the sale of dairy products,
poultry, and eggs.[14] By the end of the decade farming had definitely
become the major industry of the county.

Agriculture in Nolan County during these years continued to
follow the general pattern set in the period before 1900. Of the

[9] U.S., Department of Commerce, Bureau of the Census, *Thirteenth Census of
the United States, 1910: Population*, III, 790.

[10] The large percentage of urban increase was due to the fact that there
were no urban areas in 1900 (*ibid.*, pp. 838–839).

[11] Texas, Department of Agriculture, *Year Book, 1909*, pp. 327, 594; and
Thirteenth Census of the United States, 1910: Agriculture, VII, 693.

[12] Texas, Department of Agriculture, *Year Book, 1909*, p. 594.

[13] *Thirteenth Census of the United States, 1910: Agriculture*, VII, 693, 671.
For complete comparative data on agriculture during this period, see Appendix II.

[14] *Ibid.*, p. 671.

478,874 acres of land devoted to agriculture in 1910, only 93,296 were improved.[15] Tenancy was of growing importance, and 634 of the 1,160 farms and ranches in the county were operated by tenants. Many farms were mortgaged, but this was not unusual considering the number of new people just beginning to farm who had to borrow money at the outset. The total mortgage debt was $252,504, 21 per cent of the value of the land and buildings mortgaged.[16]

That this was an era of relative prosperity for West Texas farmers was indicated by the large rise in the amount of money invested in implements and machinery. In 1900, $22,250 was so invested, but as the use of machines on the flat land of West Texas proved profitable, this figure rose rapidly and reached $191,904 by 1910.[17] The use of farm machinery was apparently the only concession made to scientific farming and the only significant change in methods used prior to 1900; there was no money spent on fertilizer. Labor continued to be used extensively since it was necessary for the production of cotton. About one-half of the farms reported the use of hired workers, and a total of $56,000 was spent on their wages.[18]

Cereal crops and cotton were the principal money crops for Nolan County farmers, and considerably more than half of the improved acreage was devoted to their production. As more land was put into cultivation, land values increased proportionately. The average value of land per acre in 1900 was only $2.28, but by 1910 land was worth $14.98 an acre.[19]

Cattle raising continued to be an important factor in the economy, and in Nolan County the number of cattle remained between 15,000 and 20,000 throughout the decade, standing at 15,889 in 1910.[20] In that year the West Texas Cattle Raisers Association was formed in Sweetwater with Thomas Trammel, a banker and rancher of the

[15] *Ibid.*, p. 647.

[16] *Ibid.*, p. 671.

[17] *Fourteenth Census of the United States, 1920: State Compendium, Texas,* p. 124.

[18] *Thirteenth Census of the United States, 1910: Agriculture,* VII, 693.

[19] *Ibid.*, p. 647.

[20] Texas, Department of Agriculture, *Year Book, 1909,* p. 327.

community, as the first president. The purpose of the group was the general promotion of the livestock industry in West Texas, and the "establishment of a fraternal, social, and protective union" among the cattlemen of the surrounding area.[21]

Although livestock raising did not decrease in value to any appreciable extent, farming grew in importance, and in the twenty years between 1910 and 1930 the general trend toward increasing farm production typified the agricultural scene in Nolan County. There was some consolidation of farms taking place, since the number of farms and ranches dropped by 145 in the decade following 1910, and by 1930 had risen again to only 1,154, still fewer than the 1,160 in 1910.[22]

Consolidation only partially accounted for the decrease in the number of farms, for some farmers went into the army or other occupations during World War I. The impetus that United States agriculture received from the war was only partly reflected in the prosperity of West Texas farmers. Although beef and grain prices rose almost immediately after the war broke out in Europe, cotton was not so favorably affected. Moreover, production of most crops in the area increased until 1917 when a severe drought caused a temporary setback for two years.[23]

By the year following the armistice, crop production had more than recovered the losses of 1917 and 1918. That this was a period of expanding operations for farmers despite the drop in the price of cotton and the uncertainty of the weather was attested to by the increased amount of land under cultivation, by investment of $396,694 in implements and machinery, and by the valuation of Nolan County farm and ranch property in 1920 at more than $11,000,000.[24]

The value of farm products in 1920 was $5,072,471, the principal

[21] Louise Bradford, "A History of Nolan County, Texas" (Master's Thesis, University of Texas, 1950), p. 41.

[22] *Fourteenth Census of the United States, 1920: State Compendium, Texas*, p. 124; and *Fifteenth Census of the United States, 1930: Agriculture*, II, Part II, 622.

[23] *Tenth Annual Report of the Commissioner of Agriculture*, p. 322.

[24] *Fourteenth Census of the United States, 1920: State Compendium, Texas*, p. 124.

crops still being cotton and sorghums.[25] In the years following World War I there was a rapid growth of cotton production. By 1920 Nolan County farmers devoted 35,875 acres to the cultivation of that crop, and 18,124 bales were ginned during the year. At the same time production of grains was 879,868 bushels from 30,403 acres.[26] Besides crops, county farmers produced $72,683 worth of dairy products of which about one-third were sold.[27] As other phases of agriculture were increasing in value, ranching remained a profitable industry. In 1920 the 13,540 cattle and 18,529 sheep in the county were valued at just under $1,000,000.[28]

Crop production in West Texas decreased slowly from 1920 to 1923 as the area felt the effects of the national agricultural recession. However, by 1924 crop yields reached the immediate postwar level, and 1925 was a year of peak production for the decade. Between 1925 and 1930 crop raising remained in a rather static condition as insufficient rainfall made farming an uncertain occupation. In 1926 Nolan County farmers produced 19,462 bales of cotton, 9,713 bushels of corn, and 398,662 bushels of sorghum grains, with the exception of cotton a considerable drop from 1920 figures.[29]

During the late nineteen-twenties there was a movement to improve production through the use of more scientific methods. In 1928, 7,500 acres of land in Nolan County were terraced, 37 farmers practiced seed selection in order to improve crops, and 5,000 acres of pasture land were treated under a rodent campaign for the extermination of prairie dogs.[30] Although such practices helped increase production, there was little change in the economic picture for West Texas farmers.

Despite the lack of prosperity in the years preceding 1930, Nolan

[25] *Ibid.*, p. 124.

[26] *Ibid.*, p. 175.

[27] Texas, Agricultural Experiment Station, *Statistics of Texas Agriculture,* pp. 40–45.

[28] *Fourteenth Census of the United States, 1920: State Compendium, Texas,* pp. 124, 147.

[29] Texas, Agricultural Experiment Station, *Statistics of Texas Agriculture,* pp. 40–45.

[30] *West Texas Today,* IX (February, 1928), 32.

County remained a farming area, and of the 19,370 people in the county in that year, 8,475 were rural residents.[31] About one-third of the people employed in the county were engaged in agricultural occupations, the value of farm and ranch land and buildings was $13,087,747, and farmers owned machinery worth $548,804, including 113 tractors.[32] Thus farming during the decade, although maintaining its position of importance, did not make the gains registered during the 1910–1920 period.

One result of the agricultural recession was that some farmers, unable to maintain payments on their farms, became tenants. Of the 1,154 farms and ranches in the county in 1930, 665 were operated by cash or share tenants.[33] This movement was not restricted to West Texas but was general throughout the state.

Accompanying the rise in tenancy was a movement to a one-crop system. Cotton was the principal cash crop in the area, and of the 134,217 acres planted in 1930 in Nolan County, 80,232 were used for the cultivation of cotton.[34] Since weather conditions were unfavorable that year, only 10,068 bales were ginned, and the value of all crops produced dropped to $2,205,926.[35] Some of the lost income of farmers was made up by the sale of butter, poultry, and eggs which brought $330,000 in 1930.[36]

As farming temporarily decreased in importance, livestock raising made a corresponding gain. In 1930 there were 17,856 cattle and 41,181 sheep, and total livestock was valued at $1,435,388.[37] This rather substantial increase in the industry since 1920 indicated that at least a portion of the county's farmers had turned to this occupation as a means of replacing declining income from crop production.

[31] *Fifteenth Census of the United States, 1930: Agriculture*, III, Part II, 986.
[32] *Ibid.*, II, 1047; II, 1600; and I, 622.
[33] *Ibid.*, I, 622.
[34] Texas, Agricultural Experiment Station, *Statistics of Texas Agriculture*, p. 45.
[35] *Fifteenth Census of the United States, 1930: Agriculture*, II, Part II, 1482, 1571.
[36] *Ibid.*, p. 1571.
[37] *Fifteenth Census of the United States, 1930: Agriculture*, II, Part II, 1462, 1559, 1571.

Agricultural developments in Scurry County in the years between 1900 and 1930 paralleled those of Nolan County. County population in the first decade of this period grew from 4,158 to 10,924, and by 1910 the rural population was 8,410.[38] Although a variety of crops were grown during the early years of the century, cotton was fast becoming the principal crop, production rising from 900 bales in 1899 to more than 14,000 bales by 1906.[39] As late as 1909 the Texas Department of Agriculture *Year Book* reported that stock raising was the principal industry of the county, and in that year $408,748 was received from the sale of livestock.[40] However, the total value of crops in 1909 surpassed receipts from the sale of animals and stood at $639,913. The main crops raised on the 144,642 improved acres were 16,549 bushels of corn, 301,923 bushels of kaffir corn and milo maize, and 4,802 bales of cotton.[41] Tenancy was rising faster than was the total number of farms, partially because of increased emphasis on cotton production. By 1910, 909 of the 1,424 farms and ranches in the county were run by tenants.[42]

Scurry County was the only county in the area under consideration in which farmers tried to improve crop production through the use of fertilizer. In 1910, five farmers invested $212.00 in fertilizer.[43] Although there was little effort made to practice scientific farming, crop raising increased in importance in the county, and as it did there was a corresponding rise in the value of land. In 1900 land was worth $1.78 an acre, but by 1910 this figure had risen to $16.62 per acre.[44]

As in the rest of West Texas, Scurry County underwent a period of

---

[38] *Twelfth Census of the United States, 1900: Population*, I, 388; and *Thirteenth Census of the United States, 1910: Population*, III, 791, 842–843.

[39] Texas, Department of Agriculture, *Year Book, 1909*, p. 327.

[40] *Ibid.*, p. 622; and *Thirteenth Census of the United States, 1910: Agriculture*, VII, 673.

[41] *Thirteenth Census of the United States, 1910: Agriculture*, VII, 696.

[42] *Ibid.*, pp. 650, 673.

[43] This was spent for commercial fertilizer. Some use was made of barnyard fertilizer also (*ibid.*, p. 696).

[44] This figure for the price of land in 1910 was above the national average (*ibid.*, p. 650).

limited prosperity during World War I and suffered a setback in 1917 and 1918 because of the drought. In 1920 the total value of crops reached $5,677,857, land utilization being almost equally divided between cereal crops and cotton. Cotton production was 18,981 bales from 42,275 acres, and 961,640 bushels of grains were grown on 43,819 acres. Wheat had temporarily become a major crop of the county, and 64,206 bushels were harvested in 1920.[45]

This increased crop production was accomplished on fewer farms, for after rising rapidly between 1900 and 1910, the total number of farms and ranches in Scurry County dropped from 1,424 in 1910 to only 1,077 in 1920. The reduction was partially the result of consolidation since the average size of farms increased during the same period. The total value of farm and ranch property had reached $15,560,550 by 1920. This increase in property value represented a rise of more than $4,500,000 for the decade and was the result of the inflation of prices during the war period; especially inflated were prices for land, which had risen to $25.07 an acre by 1920.[46]

Scurry County remained an agricultural area throughout this period, and of the 12,217 people in the county in 1930, 9,180 were rural residents.[47] The total acreage devoted to agriculture rose substantially between 1920 and 1930, and by the latter date 92.5 per cent of the county land was in farms and ranches.[48] Despite increased acreage and a larger number of farms, production fell because of unfavorable weather conditions, and the total value of crops dropped to only $2,048,151 as a result of decreased production and lower prices.[49]

The decreasing returns from farming during the early twenties caused many farmers to turn either to ranching or to the cultivation

[45] *Fourteenth Census of the United States, 1920: State Compendium, Texas,* p. 177.

[46] *Ibid.,* p. 126.

[47] *Fifteenth Census of the United States, 1930: Population,* III, Part II, 988.

[48] These figures are misleading, for in some cases a part of the farm or ranch might be in another county, but the headquarters was in the county concerned (*Fifteenth Census of the United States, 1930: Agriculture,* II, Part II, 1378).

[49] *Ibid.,* p. 1571.

of cotton since the price of this crop remained good until about 1926. Consequently, of the 197,864 acres on which crops were harvested in 1930, 129,404 acres were devoted to the growth of cotton, and 18,235 bales were produced in that year.[50] Ranching grew in importance also, and in 1930 there were 20,288 cattle and 17,738 sheep in the county.[51]

Scurry County farmers took an action characteristic of nearly all farmers in times of low prices for staples and turned to the production of poultry and dairy products to provide cash for necessary expenses. The total value of butter and milk sold in 1930 was $108,487, and nearly $300,000 was realized from the sale of poultry and eggs.[52] Thus, at the beginning of the depression of the thirties, farmers found themselves in a rather precarious financial condition and were endeavoring to find some means of raising ready cash from their farms.

In 1900 only 37 people lived in Dawson County, and five ranches were in operation in the county.[53] Not until 1905 and 1906 when a few people began farming was there any crop production reported. In 1905 small yields of various grains were reported, and the following year 1,583 bales of cotton were produced.[54] Almost from the time of the first farm, cotton was the major crop of the county.

During the decade between 1900 and 1910 people began to move into Dawson County, and by the latter date the population was 2,320.[55] Many of these new residents were farmers, and the improved acreage in the county increased from 35 acres in 1900 to 42,631 in 1910.[56] In that year the total value of crops was $70,932. Most of

[50] Texas, Agricultural Experiment Station, *Statistics of Texas Agriculture*, p. 48.

[51] *Fifteenth Census of the United States, 1930: Agriculture*, II, Part II, 1464, 1559.

[52] *Ibid.*, p. 1571.

[53] *Fourteenth Census of the United States, 1920: State Compendium, Texas*, p. 130.

[54] Texas, Department of Agriculture, *Year Book, 1909*, p. 479.

[55] *Fourteenth Census of the United States, 1920: State Compendium, Texas*, p. 130.

[56] *Thirteenth Census of the United States, 1910: Agriculture*, VII, 637.

the grain produced was fed to cattle, for not until 1910 did a railroad reach Lamesa, the county seat, thus providing an outlet for farm production.[57]

The arrival of the Panhandle and Santa Fe Railroad in 1910, the increasing population, and the impetus given agriculture by the war caused Dawson County to become a farming area by 1920. At that time there were 574 farms and ranches in the county with property valued at $11,303,320.[58] During the war cotton had definitely become the chief crop, and 9,447 bales were ginned in 1920.[59] In addition, 112,305 bushels of corn and 476,357 tons of sorghum were harvested.[60]

Mechanization of Dawson County farms increased rapidly with the growth of cotton production. In 1900 only $2,220 was invested in implements and machinery, but by 1920 this figure had increased to $479,293, and by 1930 the county had a greater number of trucks and tractors than any of the other counties under consideration.[61]

By 1930, Dawson County, although far from the most populous, was the leading farming county in the area being studied. The application of machinery to farming on the level land of West Texas and the fertile soil of the county resulted in crop production valued at nearly $4,000,000.[62] Cotton production continued to increase, reaching a peak of 52,166 bales in 1924, and averaging about 40,000 bales each year between 1924 and 1930.[63] This dependence on one crop led to a greater number of tenants and also proved dangerous in years when there was no rain and the cotton crop failed.

[57] Bureau of Business Research, University of Texas, *An Economic Survey of Dawson County*, 1.03.

[58] *Fourteenth Census of the United States, 1920: State Compendium, Texas*, p. 113.

[59] Half of the improved acreage in the county was devoted to cotton production (*ibid.*, p. 165).

[60] *Ibid.*, p. 113; and *Fifteenth Census of the United States, 1930: Agriculture*, II, 1591–1602.

[61] *Fifteenth Census of the United States, 1930: Agriculture*, II, 1591–1602.

[62] *Ibid.*, p. 1565.

[63] Texas, Agricultural Experiment Station, *Statistics of Texas Agriculture*, pp. 43–66.

During periods of drought Dawson County had only one resource other than farming, that of ranching. Originally a ranching area entirely, stock raising maintained an important position in the economy throughout this period. The number of cattle in the county remained at about 15,000 between 1900 and 1930, and at the latter date, in addition to 16,352 cattle, there were about 1,000 sheep on Dawson County ranches.[64]

The population of Howard County, south and east of Dawson County, rose from 2,520 in 1900 to 8,881 in 1910; however, the rural increase was not as great as in the areas previously mentioned.[65] It was only in the later years of the decade that farming was of great importance in the county, for until 1905 ranching was almost the sole pursuit of rural residents. At the close of the decade stock raising was still the principal source of revenue for Howard County, but crop production was gaining rapidly.

There were 819 farms and ranches in the county in 1910, and the total value of all crops was $299,810, while receipts from the sale of livestock totaled $360,147 in the same year.[66] The principal crops, as in all of this area, were cotton and grain sorghums, and cotton ginned in 1910 amounted to 2,248 bales.[67] Although farming had developed since the turn of the century, it was still of secondary importance in the economy of the county.

The drought years during the war and consolidation by wealthier farmers made tremendous inroads in the total number of farms by 1920. Only 422 farms and ranches of the 819 in existence ten years before were still operated in 1920. Acreage under cultivation had been similarly reduced, from 853,904 acres in 1910 to only 308,678 at the end of the decade.[68]

---

[64] *Fifteenth Census of the United States, 1930: Agriculture*, II, 1453.

[65] *Twelfth Census of the United States, 1900: Population*, I, 383; and *Thirteenth Census of the United States, 1910: Population*, III, 786, 826–827. The rural increase for the decade was 89 per cent.

[66] *Thirteenth Census of the United States, 1910: Agriculture*, VII, 642, 665, 688.

[67] Texas, Department of Agriculture, *Year Book, 1909*, p. 539.

[68] *Fourteenth Census of the United States, 1920: State Compendium, Texas*, p. 118.

Despite the decrease in the number of farms and in the total acreage, crop production increased, and the value of all crops reached $2,177,089 in 1920. Cotton ginned had risen to 7,349 bales, and cereal crops totaled 383,646 bushels, including 8,816 bushels of wheat.[69] Tenancy decreased slightly during the immediate postwar years and was a little less than 50 per cent in 1920. There was an increase in mechanization of Howard County farms during the decade, for the investment in implements and machinery rose from $153,068 to $188,887 between 1910 and 1920.[70]

During the nineteen-twenties cotton was rapidly becoming the most important cash crop in the county. In 1926 production of this staple had reached 16,773 bales whereas cereal crops had dropped to less than 250,000 bushels, and there was no wheat harvested at all.[71] This trend continued; three years later 103,341 acres of land were used for the cultivation of cotton, and 17,793 bales were produced in 1929.[72]

By 1930 the population of Howard County had risen to 22,914, and there was an accompanying growth in the number of farms and ranches since 1,194 were reported being operated.[73] A great many of these new farmers were tenants, for tenancy had made substantial inroads in the preceding ten years, and 808 of the farms and ranches were so operated.[74] The rise in tenancy was partially the result of fluctuating cotton prices and partially the result of a growing dependence on cotton in the county. People who had begun to farm after the war were unable to keep their farms when the postwar price of cotton dropped, and many farmers were forced to become tenants.

The total value of crops in 1929 had fallen only slightly from the 1920 level and was $2,017,818, not a great deal more than the value of livestock, which was $1,363,696.[75] The county as a whole did not

[69] *Ibid.*, p. 169.

[70] *Ibid.*, p. 118.

[71] Texas, Agricultural Experiment Station, *Statistics of Texas Agriculture*, p. 45.

[72] *Fifteenth Census of the United States, 1930: Agriculture*, II, Part II, 1477.

[73] *Ibid., Agriculture*, I, 615; and *Population*, III, Part II, 982.

[74] *Ibid., Agriculture*, II, Part II, 1371.

[75] *Ibid.*, 1567.

suffer as great a setback in farm revenues as did the rest of the area under consideration principally because crop production had not reached a position of as great importance by 1920, and there was less to be lost than in other counties. Farmers in Howard County, as in Dawson, Nolan, and Scurry counties, turned to cotton and livestock production in the lean years of the twenties, and farming, while still important to the economy, did not continue its earlier rate of development.

In Midland and Ector counties farming did not make the gains achieved in other counties in the area. The slow population movement into the western part of the state insured the continuation of ranching as the principal agricultural industry as late as 1930. In Midland County the population grew from 1,741 in 1900 to only 8,028 thirty years later.[76] Since the county was in a semiarid part of the state, and since this period was one of limited profits from farming, it was not unusual that little progress was made in connection with crop production.

In 1909 the Texas *Year Book* of agriculture reported that a Campbell Experiment Farm, a dry-land farming experimental unit, was being operated in Midland County. The principal crops being cultivated were cotton, corn, oats, sorghum, and potatoes. The only crops reported for the county in that year were 28,198 bushels of corn and 228 bales of cotton.[77] There was also the beginning of a fairly large fruit industry in Midland County during this period, and a number of orchards were in existence. A combination of little effort to promote fruit production and the lack of irrigation caused the rather promising industry to die out. Compared to the returns from ranching, the value of crops in 1910 was insignificant. Total value of all crops for the year was $44,407, whereas $166,457 was realized from the sale of stock.[78] Almost all of the land in the county

---

[76] *Twelfth Census of the United States, 1900: Population,* I, 385; and *Fifteenth Census of the United States, 1930: Population,* III, Part II, 985.

[77] Texas, Department of Agriculture, *Year Book, 1909,* p. 583.

[78] Very little cash was received by the individual farmer for his crops since most production was consumed on the farm rather than being marketed (*Thirteenth Census of the United States, 1910: Agriculture,* VII, 693, 670).

was devoted to ranching; only 16,166 of the 466,367 acres in farms and ranches were improved.[79]

Some development of farm land in the county had taken place by 1920, and the value of crops reached $312,964, the principal production being 951 bales of cotton, 1,398 bushels of grains, and 5,987 tons of hay raised for forage.[80] At the same time the 54,782 cattle grazed on Midland County ranches were worth more than $3,000,000.[81] Ranching, rather than decreasing in importance, was becoming ever more important.

By 1930 farming on a significant scale was just beginning in Midland County. Almost all land under cultivation was used for the production of cotton, and 6,388 bales were ginned.[82] The value of farm products was rising gradually and had reached $813,161; at the same time livestock values had fallen to $1,773,265.[83] Increasing returns from crops had encouraged farmers to invest in machinery, and the total of this investment was $140,905 by 1930.[84]

The history of farming in Ector County during this thirty-year period was similar to that of Midland County. An extremely small population, only 3,958 in 1930, and a growing livestock industry that completely overshadowed farming typified the agricultural scene.[85] The first production of cotton, the major crop, was not reported until 1907 when 8 bales were ginned.[86] Two years later this figure had increased to 30 bales, and value of all crops was still less than $20,000.[87] In the same year $182,959 was received from the sale of animals, indicating that ranching was the only important agricultural industry in the county by 1910.[88]

[79] *Ibid.*, p. 642.
[80] *Fourteenth Census of the United States, 1920: State Compendium, Texas,* p. 175.
[81] *Ibid.*, p. 146.
[82] *Fifteenth Census of the United States, 1930: Agriculture,* II, Part II, 1481.
[83] *Ibid., Agriculture,* II, Part II, 1569.
[84] *Ibid., Agriculture,* I, 621.
[85] *Ibid., Population,* III, Part II, 979.
[86] Texas, Department of Agriculture, *Year Book, 1909,* p. 326.
[87] *Thirteenth Census of the United States, 1910: Agriculture,* VII, 684.
[88] *Ibid.*, p. 661.

Although the population of Ector County decreased in the decade from 1910 to 1920, from 1,178 to 760, value of farm products showed slight gains.[89] The 1920 farm crops were worth $49,821, and farmers, apparently feeling that crop production had a future in the county, had invested $42,975 in implements and machinery.[90]

During the decade following 1920 the population of the county rose, but there was very little change in the farming picture. The value of crops decreased by about $10,000 by 1930 although more crops were raised.[91] Less acreage was being devoted to the cultivation of crops, but yields were higher than the 1920 figures. Farming was never to become an important industry in Ector County, ranching continued to dominate the agricultural scene, and other industries eventually provided the greatest revenues.

The first three decades of the twentieth century were years of agricultural development and limited prosperity in Texas, and the western part of the state shared in the developments that took place. Indeed, an agricultural revolution occurred on the western plains of Texas, for at the turn of the century this area was almost completely devoted to ranching; by 1930, however, farming had not only become a major industry but had also changed from a relatively primitive occupation to a specialized and mechanized industry.

It should be remembered that production figures of farm crops were not necessarily the final measure of agricultural prosperity, for there were other factors to be considered. The amounts of various crops harvested depended on the acreage cultivated and the weather, but large production did not always mean greater profits. The 1920 crop was one of the most valuable produced during this period, but it was produced at high costs. Consequently, when prices broke sharply in the latter part of the year, actual profits were considerably reduced.[92] Furthermore, farming in West Texas was only beginning

[89] *Fourteenth Census of the United States, 1920: State Compendium, Texas,* p. 130.

[90] *Ibid.,* p. 114.

[91] *Fifteenth Census of the United States, 1930: Agriculture,* II, Part II, 1564.

[92] William Bennett Bizzell, *Rural Texas,* pp. 281–282.

to reach sizable proportions when the agricultural recession of the twenties set in.

The years of World War I were not as profitable for farmers in this area as in other parts of the United States for a variety of reasons. Wheat prices rose substantially at the outbreak of war in Europe, but wheat was a negligible crop in West Texas at the time. Although cotton prices broke sharply during the first years of the war, by 1916 they had begun to climb slowly. Cotton reached $.25 a pound at the end of 1917 and had risen to $.33 by the end of 1918. Beef prices also climbed slowly, the high for the period being reached in mid-1918.[93] But West Texas farmers were unable to take advantage of the high prices paid for their two principal products, for these were drought years on the Texas plains, and production was severely curtailed. As a result, farmers in the area did not benefit greatly from the prosperity of the war years and were not prepared for the recession of the twenties.

Although profits during the years just preceding the twenties were not large, returns from farming, when combined with rising prices during the last years of the war, were great enough to encourage many people to enter the occupation. As a result, farm indebtedness was extremely high at the time of greatest production. Credit facilities for rural residents had increased rapidly before 1920. By that date credit needs of Texas farmers were supplied by the Federal Reserve Bank in Dallas and the four joint-stock land banks, two in Dallas and one each in Houston and San Antonio, and after 1923 through the Federal Intermediate Bank in Houston.[94]

Most West Texas farmers, however, were far removed from these centers of credit and relied to a great extent on local banks and merchants for loans.[95] Nor was there much help to be secured from state agencies, for although a rural credit-union law was passed by

[93] F. A. Buechel, *Farm Cash Income in Texas, 1927–1936*, p. 10.

[94] Bizzell, *Rural Texas*, p. 287.

[95] In 1925, 41 per cent of the farmers receiving short-term credit obtained it locally from banks, 12 per cent from merchants, and 30 per cent from a combination of banks and merchants. The remaining short-term loans were obtained in a variety of combinations from loaning agencies. The usual se-

the legislature in 1913, it was relatively ineffective in providing credit facilities for rural residents.[96] Despite restrictions placed on credit, mortgages increased rapidly in the counties under consideration. In 1910 there were 680 farms and ranches mortgaged in the six counties. The total amount of the mortgages was nearly $1,500,000, 22.7 per cent of the value of the land and buildings on these farms.[97] Ten years later the number of mortgaged farms had risen to 749 although there had been little increase in the total number of farms and ranches, and by 1930 the total mortgage debt on 1,104 farms and ranches was approximately $4,500,000.[98]

Two factors contributed to the rise in the number of mortgages. First, the temptation to speculate during the war, when prices of crops and land were rising, influenced many farmers to invest in farm land in the hope of making profits by reselling. Most of these farms were mortgaged. Also, the drought of 1917–1918 caused many farmers to need cash, which they obtained by mortgaging their property. As a result, the number of mortgages increased faster than did the total number of farms during the years up to 1930.

A second form of farmer indebtedness that existed in West Texas was connected mainly with tenancy. The number of share and cash tenants in Texas had been a growing evil since the turn of the century. At that time 49.7 per cent of farms in the state were so operated, but by 1930 this figure had risen to 60.9 per cent for the state.[99] During the same period tenancy also made substantial gains in the counties under consideration. In 1900 about 20 per cent of West Texas farms were run by tenants; by 1920 the peak of 49

curity was a good reputation, endorsement by a neighbor, mortgage, or lien on crops. Most loans were for 90 to 270 days (Texas, Agricultural Experiment Station, *Short-Term Farm Credit in Texas*, pp. 5–9).

[96] Bizzell, *Rural Texas*, p. 288.

[97] *Thirteenth Census of the United States, 1910: Agriculture*, VII, 660–673.

[98] *Fifteenth Census of the United States, 1930: Agriculture*, II, Part II, 1575–1583.

[99] E. V. White and William E. Leonard, *Studies in Farm Tenancy in Texas*, p. 17; and *Fifteenth Census of the United States, 1930: Agriculture*, II, Part II, 1575–1583.

per cent had been reached, and the proportion of farms operated by tenants in the six counties in 1930 had fallen to slightly more than 41 per cent.[100] Although the figures for West Texas were considerably less than those for the whole state, some counties in the area under consideration had greater percentages. In 1930, 67 per cent of the farms in Howard County and 57 per cent of those in Nolan County were operated by tenants.[101]

West Texas differed from other cotton-producing areas in Texas in that there were few Negroes in the area. Whereas most tenants in the rest of the state were Negroes, almost all sharecroppers in West Texas were whites, and tenancy rates among whites were higher in that section than in the rest of the state. The evil of sharecropping was an almost natural accompaniment of the one-crop system prevalent in West Texas and in other parts of the state.

Between 1900 and 1930 it was virtually impossible for the share or cash tenant to become an owner of land, and any reduction in the number of tenants was usually the result of renters turning to another occupation rather than of their buying land. Most of these people were cotton farmers, and since nearly all income was received in a period of two or three months, it was necessary to find some means of obtaining credit for living expenses during the rest of the year. Such facilities were nearly always provided locally.

Most loans made to tenant farmers, and to other farmers as well, were in the form of chattel mortgages for relatively small amounts. The two chief sources of this form of credit were mercantile establishments and banks.[102] Farmers either would borrow enough money from the bank for their needs, or they would contract with a general store for farm supplies and money for running expenses. Interest rates for such loans were often more than legal rates, one reason being that the banker or merchant never knew whether or not a farmer would make a crop, and consequently whether the loan might

[100] *Fifteenth Census of the United States, 1930: Agriculture*, II, Part II, 1575–1583.

[101] *Ibid.*, pp. 1579, 1583.

[102] Bizzell, *Rural Texas*, p. 286; and White and Leonard, *Farm Tenancy*, pp. 48–54.

have to be carried over year after year. The result of the credit system was that tenants usually found themselves with no means of becoming independent.

Tenancy did not seriously affect the returns from agriculture in West Texas. Although crop production at the beginning of the century was fairly diversified, two crops, cotton and grain sorghums, soon dominated farm production in the section. The spread of cotton production into this area began early in the period, and between 1903–1907 and 1923–1927 the increase for the High Plains of Texas was from 0.2 per cent of the state's total to 4.5 per cent.[103] The increase in cotton acreage was even greater by 1929. By this time 53.9 per cent of the harvested acreage in the counties under consideration was devoted to cotton production, and the crop accounted for 56 per cent of the cash income of farmers. The tremendous increase in cotton acreage was the result of high prices during the mid-twenties and the adaptability of the West Texas soil to the crop.[104]

This growing dependence of West Texas farmers on one crop proved to be a mistake. In 1930, when almost all improved acreage was devoted to cotton, a very small crop was made because of unsatisfactory weather conditions. Also, from 1920, when the first good postwar crop was harvested, until the end of the decade prices were high in only a few years, and by 1930 had fallen to $.10 a pound.[105] Furthermore, most of the cotton was marketed in October and November, and farmers were consequently at the mercy of price fluctuations.

To avoid the inconsistencies of price some attempts were made at cooperative marketing. In 1920 the Farm Bureau Federation asked Aaron Shapiro, a California lawyer, to assist in working out a marketing plan for Texas farmers.[106] The result was the formation of a number of cooperatives based on commodities rather than on

[103] Elmer H. Johnson, *The Basis of the Commercial and Industrial Development of Texas*, p. 69.

[104] Buechel, *Farm Cash Income in Texas*, pp. 9, 13.

[105] *Ibid.*, p. 43.

[106] Shapiro had made a study of Danish cooperative marketing and had for

regions. There was some success during the first years of the movement. In 1920 members of the Howard County Marketing Association, a branch of the Texas Farm Bureau Federation, reported the sale of 850 bales of cotton for from $7.50 to $12.50 more than most farmers were getting.[107] In September and October 1921 a second marketing association, the Howard County Farm Labor Union, sold 1,544 bales of cotton for $169,843.87.[108] By 1930 cooperative marketing and purchasing was still utilized but was of minor importance. In that year 104 farmers in the six counties sold crops for about $75,000 through cooperative groups.[109]

Almost as important to West Texas farmers as cotton were grain sorghums. These plants were first introduced into the area about 1887, and by 1921 West Texas produced nearly one-half of all the sorghums grown in the United States. Milo maize accounted for about 75 per cent of the sorghum produced in the area, and the remainder was about equally divided between kaffir corn and feterita, which had originally been developed in connection with the livestock industry and were usually bundled for feed.[110] By 1930, 34.4 per cent of harvested acreage in the area under consideration was devoted to sorghum, but this crop accounted for only 4.5 per cent of the cash income since a great deal of the production was used for feed.[111]

Important to the production of crops in West Texas was experimentation carried on by various Texas Agricultural Experiment Stations, both in the area itself and at College Station. Tests carried out at stations like the one at Big Spring helped farmers obtain the

------

a number of years been legal representative for cooperative marketing groups in California (Bizzell, *Rural Texas*, p. 295).

[107] *Big Spring* (Texas) *Herald,* January 21, 1921. Howard County Wool Growers had also formed a cooperative, which shipped wool to Philadelphia for sale (*ibid.*, April 1, 1921).

[108] *Ibid.*, September 23 and October 7, 1921.

[109] *Fifteenth Census of the United States, 1930: Agriculture,* II, Part II, 1591–1602.

[110] Bizzell, *Rural Texas,* 188–189.

[111] Buechel, *Farm Cash Income in Texas,* p. 9.

greatest yield per acre.[112] Other experiments, performed mainly during the late twenties, led to the development of new plants, such as storm-resistant cotton; they showed farmers the best use of some plants and demonstrated the best use of fertilizer in farming.[113]

Perhaps most important of the tests conducted were those connected with cotton production. In the years following 1925 the extensive use of machines on cotton acreage was principally the result of experiments made by the various stations. It was discovered that the cotton planter was effective on the plains of West Texas, and the two-row riding planter was used in most of the area.[114] Harvesting cotton by mechanical means also was found to be profitable, and the stripper and picker were both adopted to some extent before the large-scale development of storm-resistant plants.[115] Mechanization of West Texas farms increased rapidly as new methods were discovered, and by 1930 there were 413 tractors in the counties under consideration.[116]

In addition to crop production, which was dominated by cotton and sorghums, West Texas was still dependent to some extent on the livestock industry for agricultural income. In 1930, 126,652 cattle and 67,110 sheep were still on the ranches of the six counties.[117]

[112] In the period between 1914 and 1921 production of crops at the Big Spring Station was: cotton, .33 bale per acre average; milo, 27 bushels per acre; kaffir, 19.4 bushels per acre; and June corn, 8.9 bushels per acre (*Big Spring Herald*, September 23, 1921).

[113] Texas, Agricultural Experiment Station, *Large Scale Cotton Production in Texas*; *Commercial Fertilizers in 1924–1925*; *Commercial Fertilizers in 1928–1929 and Their Uses*; and *Sudan Grass for Hay, Seed, and Pasture*.

[114] Texas, Agricultural Experiment Station, *Calibration of Cotton Planting Mechanisms*, p. 9; and *The Effect of Spacing on the Yield of Cotton*, p. 14.

[115] The stripper was used more widely than the picker, but most picking was done by Mexican laborers. The use of mechanical pickers was not very successful with storm-resistant cotton (Texas, Agricultural Experiment Station, *Mechanical Harvesting of Cotton in Northwest Texas*, pp. 19, 31; *The Mechanical Harvesting of Cotton*, pp. 16–17; and *Mechanized Production of Cotton in Texas*, pp. 8–9, 36–37).

[116] *Fifteenth Census of the United States, 1930: Agriculture*, II, Part II, 1453–1464.

[117] *Ibid.*

Although stock raising had decreased in relative importance, the
industry had changed little in size during the thirty-year period.
The last of the big ranches had been cut up into farms by 1930, and
ranching, like farming, was becoming a more specialized pursuit as
the breeding of fine herds became more important.

Few urban centers existed in West Texas to offer relief from the
drudgery of rural life, but the farmer's lot was not all bad. Some
aspects of modern life were beginning to appear on farms in the
region, and of the 4,342 farms and ranches in the counties being
considered, nearly 21 per cent had telephones and a little over 5
per cent had electricity in their homes. About one-fifth of the farmers
had water piped to their houses, but only half of this number had
water piped to their bathrooms.[118] Farm life in West Texas had only
partially benefited from the technological developments made during
the century. Despite the lack of modern conveniences, there was
little difference between urban and country life in the area, and
consequently there was little unfavorable comparison to be made.
This region was on the verge of a period of growth and expansion,
but this development was not to be primarily the result of agricultural
prosperity.

[118] *Fifteenth Census of the United States, 1930: Agriculture*, II, Part II,
1591–1602.

CHAPTER FIVE

URBAN GROWTH, 1900–1930

W EST TEXAS was primarily an agricultural region in the period before 1930, and the towns in the area were at first small market villages serving the farmers of the surrounding countryside. In each county only one important town developed, the county seat, and there the economic, social, and cultural life of the farmers was centered. A few smaller towns started during these early years of the twentieth century, but they did not grow to any extent since the county life was so dominated by the seats of county government.

Typical of the towns that began and later failed around the turn of the century was the small community of Soash, Howard County. This settlement was the promotional scheme of three land speculators who contracted with Colonel C. C. Slaughter for 150,000 acres of land to be sold to settlers.[1] Plans were made to run two excursion trains each day to Big Spring where prospective settlers would be met and taken by wagon to the townsite. The town was started, a few brick buildings were constructed, and then the whole undertaking collapsed because the settlers did not come. There were no rail connections to the site, and the proposed building of a spur line did

---

[1] John Allison Rickard, "The Ranch Industry of the Texas South Plains" (Master's Thesis, University of Texas, 1927), pp. 155–156; and Texas, Department of Agriculture, *Year Book, 1909*, p. 539.

not take place. The county seat with its railroad was too convenient for farmers to support a rival and out-of-the-way market.[2]

Big Spring remained the only town of consequence in Howard County because of its adequate transportation facilities and because the county's limited population could not support another urban development. In 1900 the county population was only 2,520, about 1,400 of whom lived in the county seat.[3] At the time, the town and county were served by a daily and a weekly newspaper. In 1898 W. V. Irvin started the *Big Spring Enterprise,* a weekly paper that was published until 1911. The *Daily Venture* was begun in 1899 but lasted only a few years since the town was not large enough to support a daily paper. A second weekly, the *Big Spring Herald,* began publication in 1904 and in 1928 became a daily that has been published since that time.[4] Thus the county, since the late nineteenth century, was served by publications that carried the news of the area to its residents.

Other signs that the town was growing were the presence of two banks. The First National, organized in 1890, and the West Texas National, which was begun in 1902, were united after the Panic of 1907 when it appeared they might fail as separate institutions.[5] The State National Bank was chartered in March 1909, and in that year the town's banks had capital totaling $360,000 and deposits of $684,000.[6]

As early as 1900 there was also some manufacturing in Howard County, for the census of that year reported eleven manufacturing establishments with products valued at $155,440. Seventy-four employees were hired by these companies, and total wages were

[2] Another example of the small town that failed to grow was Coahoma, which in 1930 still had only 620 residents (U.S., Department of Commerce, Bureau of the Census, *Fifteenth Census of the United States, 1930: Population,* I, 1074).

[3] *Twelfth Census of the United States, 1900: Population,* I, 383.

[4] John R. Hutto, *Howard County in the Making,* no page.

[5] *Big Spring* (Texas) *Herald,* April 6, 1938.

[6] Texas, Department of Agriculture, *Year Book, 1909,* p. 539.

$53,460.[7] Most of these plants were food-processing or agriculture-connected establishments, and cotton gins accounted for the majority of the business. Between 1900 and 1930 manufacturing became an essential part of the county's economy, and gypsum and oil-related industries supplanted agriculture-connected products in importance. By 1930 products valued at $9,882,521 were being produced by industries that employed 504 wage earners at total wages of $817,235.[8]

The principal industry of Big Spring was the Texas and Pacific Railroad shop, which employed about 250 people. Consequently, there was considerable apprehension among townspeople in 1921 when it was announced that the shops would be closed indefinitely. The company issued a statement that the layoff was the result of "the necessity of further retrenchment by the road," and not of the rejection of a proposed wage cut by employees.[9] Whatever the reason for the reduction in the labor force, it was a serious situation for the town, because the Texas and Pacific payroll in Big Spring averaged about $60,000 a month.[10] Instead of actually closing the shops, the railroad laid off 114 of their employees during April 1921.[11] Throughout the summer most of these men were unable to find permanent jobs, but in August, 39 men were rehired by the Texas and Pacific.[12]

Aside from unusual situations such as this one, unemployment was a rare occurrence in Howard County because there was little industry and little chance of layoffs. In 1929 out of a county population of 22,888, only 448 people were unemployed and looking for

---

[7] *Twelfth Census of the United States, 1900: Manufactures*, p. 870.

[8] *Fifteenth Census of the United States, 1930: Manufactures*, III, 508.

[9] *Big Spring Herald*, April 22, 1921.

[10] *Ibid.*, September 2, 1921.

[11] *Ibid.*, April 29, 1921.

[12] *Ibid.*, July 15, 1921. In October fourteen more men were rehired (*ibid.*, October 7, 1921). During the summer of 1921 the labor situation was complicated when "many people" began to come to Big Spring where some road work was being done. The newspaper warned that there was more than enough local labor, and that the newcomers would be stranded (*ibid.*, July 15, 1921).

a job, and 89 had jobs but were temporarily laid off.[13] The majority of the unemployed, 352, were in Big Spring where greater job opportunity existed.[14]

Of the people employed at this time, about one-fifth were engaged in agriculture. Wholesale and retail trade, the oil industry, railroads, and building trades accounted for most of the remainder.[15] As long as Howard County continued to be predominately a farming area, there was little serious trouble concerning unemployment.

People moving into West Texas apparently brought with them a desire to have their children educated, and schools were among the first permanent buildings constructed. Although the first Big Spring school building was completed in 1882, just about a year after the town was settled, and a number of others were built before 1900, the Big Spring Independent School District was not created until 1901.[16] In that year the citizens of the town approved two bond issues totaling $21,000 for the construction of schools.[17] In 1909, when the county scholastic population was 2,016, 71 per cent of the children between the ages of six and fourteen went to school.[18] The percentage of attendance remained high in both the town and county as a whole except for those over eighteen years of age. By 1930, 88.9 per cent of the children in the county and 92.3 per cent of those in Big Spring remained in school until the age of thirteen.[19] During this period public education was well supported by the people of Howard County.

One need of Big Spring residents was not as easy to provide for as was an adequate school system. Although one reason for choosing the

[13] *Fifteenth Census of the United States, 1930: Unemployment,* I, 994.

[14] *Ibid.,* p. 997.

[15] Of the 8,542 people employed in the county, 1,722 were engaged in agriculture (*ibid., Occupations,* III, Part II, 1039).

[16] Hutto, *Howard County,* no page; and *Big Spring Herald,* April 6, 1938.

[17] *Big Spring Herald,* April 6, 1938.

[18] *Thirteenth Census of the United States, 1910: Population,* III, 827.

[19] Within the county as a whole, 84.5 per cent of those in the fourteen- to fifteen-year age group, 51 per cent of the sixteen- to seventeen-year group, and 15.8 per cent of the eighteen- to twenty-year group were in school. The figures for Big Spring were about 3 per cent higher in each group (*Fifteenth Census of the United States, 1930: Population,* III, Part II, 982, 1007).

site of the town had been the presence of a satisfactory water supply nearby, as early as 1886 the commissioners court contracted for the drilling of an artesian well to supplement the water supply of the big spring. The original appropriation of $3,000 was not enough, and in 1893 an additional $500 was spent, but after reaching a depth of 1,440 feet, the attempt to find water was abandoned.[20] During the early years of the century a few small wells were completed, but by 1921 the town had outgrown these facilities.

On April 2, 1921, an election was held, and a bond issue of $65,000 was approved to complete improvements on a municipal waterworks system.[21] This would include drilling a well and building a reservoir with a capacity of 1,500,000 gallons. By September of that year the local press reported that the water situation had become critical since there were some difficulties in completing the well, and that no solution to the water shortage was apparent.[22] Two months later the headlines proclaimed "Abundant Water Supply Assured"; the well had been finished and flowed 5,800 gallons an hour.[23] The boast of the paper was true only for the immediate future, for Big Spring was later to need additional water facilities.

The citizens of the Howard County seat were willing to spend money for a necessity such as water improvement, but aside from this there was little evidence of public spirit. During 1920 and 1921 the *Big Spring Herald* undertook a campaign to obtain a city sewer system without success, and Big Spring continued to rely on cesspools until the thirties.[24] A plan to gravel the dusty streets of the town was similarly unsuccessful, for a majority of property owners in the business district refused to pay the $.50 per front foot assessment that was required for the improvement.[25]

Little in the way of entertainment existed in Big Spring, and in this respect the community was still a small country town. A great deal of excitement was generated in the town in 1901 after the state legislature passed the act that allowed individuals to homestead four sections of land. On the day appointed for filing claims, lines formed

[20] Hutto, *Howard County*, no page.
[21] *Big Spring Herald*, April 8, 1921.
[22] *Ibid.*, September 16, 1921.
[23] *Ibid.*, November 18, 1921.
[24] *Ibid.*, October 21, 1921.
[25] *Ibid.*, September 16, 1921.

at the land office, cowboys and farmers fought it out with their fists, and in the end the cowboys emerged victorious.[26] Less exciting, but probably more entertaining, were bond elections, political contests, and the Chautauqua programs that made an annual trip into West Texas. The Chautauqua presented a varied fare including lecturers, light opera, a singing band, a ladies orchestra, a dramatic company, and a violinist.[27]

The town of Big Spring developed slowly during the first years of the twentieth century. Not until 1904 was a petition circulated calling for an election on the question of incorporation of the community. The petition was presented to the commissioners court in 1906, and the following year an election was held in which the voters approved incorporation, 132 to 85.[28] A mayoral-aldermanic type of city government was instituted and continued until 1927, when it was superceded by the commission form of government with administration by a city manager.[29]

Because the Texas and Pacific shops were located in Big Spring, there were generally more jobs available than in other towns in the area. As a result, many people were attracted to the town, and the urban population, in relation to the rural, was greater in Howard County than in most of the area under consideration. The population of Big Spring, which increased from 4,102 in 1910 to 13,735 in 1930, also had a comparatively large proportion of foreign-born persons for a West Texas community.[30] The number of foreigners, most of whom were employed by the railroad, was 357 in 1910, but by 1930 had decreased to 113.[31]

At the end of this period Big Spring was a growing country town. It was dependent to a large extent on the trade of farmers in Howard County and served as a shipping point for most of the agricultural

[26] Hutto, *Howard County*, no page.

[27] *Big Spring Herald*, March 11, 1921.

[28] Hutto, *Howard County*, no page.

[29] *Big Spring Herald*, April 6, 1938.

[30] *Thirteenth Census of the United States, 1910: Population*, III, 855; and *Fifteenth Census of the United States, 1930: Population*, I, 34.

[31] *Thirteenth Census of the United States, 1910: Population*, III, 855; and *Fifteenth Census of the United States, 1930: Population*, III, Part II, 1007.

products of the county. The town was fortunate in having a second industry in the form of the railroad shops, which provided a dependable payroll that was spent in the town. By 1930 a new industry, oil, was just beginning in Big Spring, but its full effect was not felt until later.

Sweetwater, county seat of Nolan County, although settled about the same time as Big Spring, did not develop quite as rapidly. Sweetwater was also principally dependent on the rural population of the county for business. The earliest bank in the town was organized in 1883 by Thomas Trammell largely as a credit facility for Nolan County farmers. This institution, which originally had capital of $15,000, failed in 1908. By that time the First National Bank had been started, and in 1909 the Farmer's and Merchant's Bank and Trust Company was formed with capital of $78,000.[32] By 1925 Nolan County was served by six banks, three of them located in Sweetwater.[33]

Bank failures in Sweetwater were not unknown, but the history of newspapers in the town showed an even greater variety of success and failure. The first paper begun in the county managed to continue publication for eight years, from 1882 to 1890.[34] In 1897 a weekly paper appeared, the *Sweetwater Reporter*. In 1911 and 1912 the *Reporter* was printed as a daily, but it was not well supported in a town the size of Sweetwater, which had about 4,300 people at that time.[35] Publication of the *Reporter* was suspended altogether in the fall of 1912 and was not resumed until 1914.[36] During the war the paper continued to appear, and then in 1919 it failed for the second time. In March 1920 the *Sweetwater Reporter* once again began publication and has continued since that time. Various other newspapers in Nolan County had difficulties and were forced to suspend publication. The *Sweetwater Weekly Sun* lasted from 1909 to 1910,

[32] Louise Bradford, "A History of Nolan County, Texas" (Master's Thesis, The University of Texas, 1934), pp. 63–64.

[33] Tax Assessor's Roll for Nolan County, Texas, State Archives, Records Division, Austin, Texas.

[34] Bradford, "History of Nolan County," p. 60.

[35] *Ibid.*, p. 61.

[36] *Ibid.*; and *Sweetwater* (Texas) *Reporter*, March 7, 1936.

and the *Sweetwater Signal* appeared in 1910 and lasted for one year.[37]

During its early history the Nolan County seat was apparently plagued by unsuccessful business ventures and various wildcat schemes. In 1897 Irving Wheatcroft began selling bonds to the citizens of Sweetwater for the Colorado Valley Railroad Company. After the grading had been completed to the first town and eight miles of track had been laid, Wheatcroft disappeared.[38] The company was reorganized by the people of the community as the Panhandle and Gulf Railroad, and the tangible assets of the company, eight miles of track, twenty miles of grading, and considerable right of way, were sold to A. E. Stilwell, who announced that the Kansas City, Mexico, and Orient Railroad would come through Sweetwater.[39]

Construction was finally started in 1903 after the citizens of Sweetwater agreed to purchase stock in one of Stilwell's construction companies.[40] By 1908 through service between Sweetwater and Kansas City had been established. Shortly after 1910 the railroad moved its general offices and shops from Sweetwater to San Angelo, and although Sweetwater obtained an injunction to prevent the transfer on the grounds of prior agreements, the case was lost by the town when taken to the state supreme court.[41] In 1928 the Orient went into receivership, and was taken over by the Atchison, Topeka, and Santa Fe.

Two other railroads made stops in Sweetwater. In 1906 the Roscoe, Snyder, and Pacific was begun.[42] Original plans were for the road to make connections at the New Mexico border which would give access to the West Coast, but the line never got beyond Fluvania, about 50 miles northwest of Sweetwater. Despite this fact, the line was a profitable one from the time of its inception. The last railroad

[37] Bradford, "History of Nolan County," p. 61; and *Sweetwater Reporter*, March 7, 1936.

[38] Bradford, "History of Nolan County," p. 49.

[39] *Ibid.*, p. 51. The Panhandle and Gulf only tried to dispose of their holdings to prevent the loss from being too great.

[40] Texas, Department of Agriculture, *Year Book, 1909*, p. 594.

[41] Bradford, "History of Nolan County," pp. 52–53.

[42] *Ibid.*; and Texas, Department of Agriculture, *Year Book, 1909*, p. 594.

built into Sweetwater was the Atchison, Topeka, and Santa Fe in 1911,[43] and the Santa Fe shops in Sweetwater were a contributing factor to the growth of the town.

One necessity for the railroads, as for the town, was an abundant supply of water. Although the community was located on Sweetwater Creek, this source proved inadequate as the population grew, and in 1885 the county commissioners appropriated $800.00 for the construction of a public well and a sixteen-foot windmill on the courthouse square. When completed, the well cost $1,300, the balance having been subscribed by the townspeople. This well supplied the water needs of the town until 1898 when a $10,000 bond issue was approved by the town council for the construction of a lake and a water supply system.[44] To help pay off the debt, a contract was signed between the town and the Colorado Valley Railroad providing that the road would purchase water for its locomotives from the city water system.[45]

Plans for the new facilities progressed rapidly. The bonds were sold to F. R. Fulton and Company of Chicago, a contract for building the lake was let to J. B. Oldham of Dallas, and 34 acres of land were purchased from J. H. Weisacre for $3,000 for a lakesite north of the town. Then, before plans could be carried out, litigation arose, and in 1899 the Nolan County District Court ruled the incorporation of Sweetwater invalid, thus destroying the town government.[46]

For three years there was no municipal government in Sweetwater until a second incorporation was approved in 1902. During this period the town relied on the public well for its water supply, and repairs were made on the well in 1903. In 1908 R. C. Crane conducted a campaign for the organization of a local water company, and through public subscription the water plant was finally completed.[47]

---

[43] Bradford, "History of Nolan County," p. 54.
[44] *Sweetwater Reporter*, March 7, 1936.
[45] Bradford, "History of Nolan County," p. 77.
[46] *Ibid.*
[47] R. C. Crane, "Early Days in Sweetwater," *West Texas Historical Association Year Book*, VIII (June, 1932), 46.

In 1914 the city council voted to issue $50,000 in bonds for the construction of a reservoir. After approval by the electorate, Lake Trammell was built, but since it often became dry during the summer months, it was still necessary to pipe water from Roscoe, about ten miles away, where Sweetwater had twenty windmills in operation. A further attempt to solve the water problem was made in 1925 with the construction of Lake Sweetwater, but unfortunately the project did not provide adequate funds to pipe the water into the city.[48] Consequently, water was still being piped from Roscoe in 1930.

Before an adequate water supply had been provided for Sweetwater, a fire broke out in the town's business district in 1902. The courthouse pump was the only available water supply; a bucket brigade was formed, and wet blankets were spread on the roofs of buildings to prevent the fire from spreading to other wooden structures in the area.[49] A few months later a second fire broke out and destroyed most of the buildings saved in the first disaster. As a result of these fires brick buildings replaced most of the stores destroyed in the commercial section of town. The rebuilding after the fire caused Sweetwater to take on some aspects of a modern town long before other towns in the area made similar improvements.

In 1915 the first paving, crushed rock, was put down in Sweetwater.[50] Ten years later $116,888 was spent for "Bitulithic" paving for several blocks of the main streets.[51] Coal was most commonly used for heating purposes in Sweetwater until after the discovery of oil in West Texas. In 1927 the Community Natural Gas Company purchased gas from West Texas fields and piped it to Sweetwater.[52]

A few minor industries were also attracted to the town at a relatively early date. A cotton gin was built by N. I. Dulaney, a local merchant, as early as 1888.[53] In 1904 a cottonseed-oil mill was con-

[48] Bradford, "History of Nolan County," p. 82.
[49] Crane, "Early Days in Sweetwater," p. 36.
[50] *Sweetwater Reporter*, September 28, 1941.
[51] *Big Spring Herald*, December 11, 1925.
[52] *Sweetwater Reporter*, September 28, 1941.
[53] *Ibid.*

structed to take advantage of the growing importance of cotton production on county farms. The capital stock of $50,000 was subscribed by the residents of Sweetwater, and in addition to the oil plant, this corporation purchased a cotton gin established four years earlier.[54]

The people of the town were again called upon in 1910 to aid in financing a packing plant, a branch of the McSweeny Packing Company of New Jersey. The agreement called for the assistance of the townspeople in building the plant, the promise of municipal authorities that no other packing company would be allowed in the city, and the provision of 100 acres of municipal land for the facilities.[55] Shortly after the four-story brick building was completed and machinery installed, a fire destroyed the plant. However, it was rebuilt, and other packing companies were later attracted to Sweetwater despite the agreement signed with the McSweeny company.

The most important industry established in Sweetwater attempted to take advantage of the natural resources of the surrounding countryside. Nolan County was the site of excellent deposits of gypsum rock and gypsite, an unusual mixture of gypsum and clay. In 1923 the United States Gypsum Company built a plant at Sweetwater that was subsequently enlarged a number of times.[56] The payroll of this industry was eventually to provide the greatest single source of income for the merchants of the community.

By 1930 there were eighteen manufacturing establishments of various kinds in Nolan County. The 351 employees of these plants received annual pay of more than $500,000, and the total value of manufactured products was $4,385,844.[57] Because of the presence of these industrial plants in the area, there was little unemployment. In late 1929 only 404 people were out of work and seeking jobs out of a county population of 19,323.[58]

The population of Sweetwater grew rapidly during the first thirty

[54] Bradford, "History of Nolan County," pp. 42–43.
[55] *Sweetwater Reporter*, September 28, 1941.
[56] *Ibid.*, August 13, 1954.
[57] *Fifteenth Census of the United States, 1930: Manufactures*, III, 508.
[58] *Ibid., Unemployment*, I, 996.

years of the twentieth century, rising more quickly than the rural population of Nolan County. In 1900 there were 2,611 people living in the county, 670 of them in Sweetwater.[59] The greatest growth of the area took place during the next decade as people moved into West Texas in fairly large numbers, and in 1910 the population of Sweetwater was 4,176 and that of the county was 11,999.[60]

Because of the rapid growth of population in West Texas, a meeting of representatives from various counties in the region was held at Sweetwater in the spring of 1921. They demanded that the state be redistricted so the newly developed western portion might have more adequate representation in the state legislature.[61] This plea might have had more effect ten years before when the population was growing very fast, but in the decade between 1910 and 1920 the percentage of increase was small. In any case, the request fell on deaf ears and no attempt to comply with it was made at the time.

Following World War I the population movement into West Texas began again, and by 1930 there were 19,370 people in Nolan County. The greatest portion of the increase was in Sweetwater, whose population was 10,848.[62] One other town, Roscoe, which had 1,250 residents, existed in the county.[63] Thus Nolan County, although still basically a farming area, had a greater urban population than it did rural by 1930. Sweetwater had attracted enough industry and mercantile facilities to insure a reasonably heavy demand for labor. At the same time, returns from farming were growing smaller in the years from 1920 to 1930, and rural life simply was not as inviting as it had been in previous years.

With the exception of Big Spring and Sweetwater, there was little development of towns in the area under consideration before 1930. Scurry County, north and slightly west of Nolan County, was an area most suitable for farming and stock raising, and little else in the way of industry appeared in the county. In 1890 the census reported that

[59] *Twelfth Census of the United States, 1900: Population,* I, 386.

[60] *Thirteenth Census of the United States, 1910: Population,* III, 790.

[61] *Big Spring Herald,* April 8, 1921.

[62] *Fifteenth Census of the United States, 1930: Population,* III, Part II, 986.

[63] *Ibid., Population,* I, 1080.

there were four manufacturing establishments in the county capital-ized at $3,160, but no subsequent growth along these lines took place.[64] In 1910 there were six plants with products valued at $10,095 and with only seven wage earners other than clerical work-ers.[65] By 1930 seven establishments were listed, and the value of their products had risen to just over $250,000. Since only 30 employees were hired in these plants, and since the annual payroll was $26,906, the effect on the economy of the county was not great.[66] Throughout the period the manufacturing establishments were usually connected with agriculture, and most were cotton gins.

The town of Snyder grew slowly during these years because its only reason for existence was as a seat of county government and as a trading center for the rural population of Scurry County. The town was incorporated in 1907, and by 1910 had 2,514 residents, a number that changed little between that time and 1930, when the population was only 3,008.[67] At that time there were five banks in the county, four of them in Snyder, with deposits of $508,925.[68] These institutions were almost completely dependent on financial transactions with farmers for their existence.

Snyder lacked adequate transportation facilities, and this was probably the principal reason for its slow growth. Whereas the towns south of Scurry County were located on the main branch of the Texas and Pacific, the sole line passing through Snyder was the Roscoe, Snyder, and Pacific, which made local connections only.[69] Even after connections were later made with the Texas and Pacific at Roscoe, it was still more convenient for farmers in the southern part of the county to take their produce and cattle to Sweetwater or Colorado City for shipment.

[64] *Eleventh Census of the United States, 1890: Report of Manufactures*, I, 604–605.

[65] *Twelfth Census of the United States, 1900: Manufactures*, II, 870.

[66] *Fifteenth Census of the United States, 1930: Manufactures*, III, 509.

[67] *Thirteenth Census of the United States, 1910: Population*, III, 791; and *Fifteenth Census of the United States, 1930: Population*, III, Part II, 988.

[68] Texas, Department of Agriculture, *Year Book, 1909*, p. 622.

[69] In 1925 the Roscoe, Snyder, and Pacific built a depot in Snyder (*Big Spring Herald*, December 11, 1925).

There was little difficulty in obtaining sufficient water for the needs of Snyder because the town remained small. The Colorado River lay in the southern part of the county, and the county seat was located on Deep Creek. In addition, water was fairly easily obtainable from wells. Consequently, no attempt was made to establish a municipal water system during the early years, and each citizen had to provide water for his needs.

Although most people in Scurry County were rural residents, a school system was established, and the percentage of students in attendance was high until the eighteen- to twenty-year age group was reached.[70] At that age the young people of the county were usually beginning to establish homes of their own. The percentage of children under fifteen years of age attending school rose from 81.5 in 1910 to nearly 90 in 1930. In the sixteen- to seventeen-year age group only 48.7 per cent attended school in 1920, but by the end of the decade, 72 per cent were in classes.[71]

As Scurry County grew, it changed very little, remaining an agricultural region. The county population rose from 4,158 in 1900 to 12,188 in 1930, and at the latter date the rural population was 9,180.[72] Of the 3,863 workers in the county, nearly two-thirds were engaged in farming or ranching.[73] Beside Snyder, only one other town existed in Scurry County in 1930, the village of Hermleigh, which had a population of 544.[74]

Snyder was a typical, rather unprogressive, West Texas farm and ranch town. The population was predominantly white, there being only 27 Negroes, and the residents were nearly all natives (only 7

[70] Only 15.1 per cent of those between eighteen and twenty years were attending school in 1920, and in 1930 the percentage was 24.6 (*Fourteenth Census of the United States, 1920: Population*, III, 1010; and *Fifteenth Census of the United States, 1930: Population*, III, Part II, 988).

[71] *Thirteenth Census of the United States, 1910: Population*, III, 791; and *Fifteenth Census of the United States, 1930: Population*, III, Part II, 988.

[72] *Twelfth Census of the United States, 1900: Population*, I, 388; and *Fifteenth Census of the United States, 1930: Population*, III, Part II, 988.

[73] *Fifteenth Census of the United States, 1930: Population*, III, Part II, 1050.

[74] *Ibid., Population*, I, 1082.

foreign-born whites lived in the county seat).[75] The townspeople were not very prosperous, and although the majority of them owned their own homes, 449 families of the 763 in town, the average value of those homes was only $2,322.[76] Tenants in the county paid an average of $14.58 a month for their dwellings.[77] At the close of this period there was nothing to indicate that Snyder or Scurry County would ever cease to be wholly dependent on agriculture in a period when farming and stock raising were not particularly profitable.

Dawson County, west of Scurry County, was extremely slow in developing. When Frank Connor, an employee on the Slaughter ranch, organized a townsite company in 1903 and surveyed the site of Lamesa, there were only about 50 people living in the county, most of whom were ranch employees.[78] The county was entirely devoted to ranching and was controlled by the ranch owners. Dawson County was almost completely isolated because of the lack of transportation facilities, and ranchers hauled supplies by wagon and team from Big Spring or Colorado City.[79] The first post office was established at the Godair and Bishop Ranch before Lamesa was settled.[80] Mail was delivered to the ranch twice a week by muleteam. Not until 1910, when the Panhandle and Santa Fe Railroad extended a line to Lamesa, was the county seat connected to markets by rail.

Schools were among the first structures built in Lamesa, and the year following the establishment of the town, a one-room frame building was used as a school.[81] In 1910 a four-room building was used as an elementary school, and during the twenties a new elementary school and a high school were constructed at a cost of $210,000.[82] School attendance in Lamesa and Dawson County was much the same as in the other counties in the area. The children

[75] *Ibid., Population,* III, Part II, 1013.

[76] *Ibid., Families,* VI, 1324, 1299.

[77] *Ibid.,* p. 1299.

[78] *Midland* (Texas) *Reporter Telegram,* March 9, 1952.

[79] Bureau of Business Research, University of Texas, *An Economic Survey of Dawson County,* 1.03.

[80] *Ibid.*

[81] *Midland Reporter Telegram,* March 9, 1952.

[82] The elementary school was built in 1921, the high school in 1924 (*ibid.*).

usually remained in classes until seventeen or eighteen years of age when they began to set up their own homes and started farming.

The percentage of population increase between 1900 and 1910 was great since there was almost no population in 1900, but not too many people actually came into the county. In 1910 there were 2,320 residents in the county, and by 1920, 4,309 people resided in Dawson County and 1,188 in Lamesa.[83] The period of greatest development for this county was between 1920 and 1930, for at the latter date the county population was 13,573, and Lamesa had 3,528 people.[84] The high proportion of rural residents indicated the agricultural nature of the life and economy of the county.

Lamesa, perhaps more than any other town in the area under consideration, showed few signs of modern development by 1930. During the twenties gas was brought into the community from oil fields in West Texas, and an electric plant was started, but aside from these evidences of progress there was little change in the town.[85] As the town grew, a few more stores were opened and some cotton gins were built, but Lamesa remained a small country town catering to the needs of farmers and ranchers in the county.

Throughout the period before 1930, Midland County remained primarily an urban area as far as population distribution was concerned. The county population rose from 1,741 in 1900 to only 8,028 in 1930, but at the latter date there were 5,484 people living in the town of Midland.[86] Urban development was stimulated because the county was almost entirely devoted to livestock raising and because farming was just beginning at the end of the period. Consequently, there were few rural residents. Also, there was some minor industry in Midland, and the oil business was already attracting many people to the town.

As early as 1900 the census reported that there were twelve manufacturing establishments in Midland producing goods worth $20,-

[83] *Fourteenth Census of the United States, 1920: Population,* I, 130.

[84] *Fifteenth Census of the United States, 1930: Population,* III, Part II, 978.

[85] Bureau of Business Research, University of Texas, *An Economic Survey of Dawson County,* 1.03.

[86] *Fifteenth Census of the United States, 1930: Population,* III, Part II, 985; and *Twelfth Census of the United States, 1900: Population,* I, 385.

596.[87] Among these businesses was a mill to grind cereals and feed-stuffs and a broom factory, both of which later failed.[88] The inability of these industries to make profits did not deter other businessmen, and in 1909 there was a cement-block factory and an ice plant in the small town. At that time the community had three banks with capital of $335,000 and deposits of $776,000.[89] Small manufacturing, though not then a major factor in the economy, did provide some diversification of industry for the county. At the end of World War I a few cotton gins had been built, and there were seven manufacturing establishments employing seventeen workers for total annual wages of $18,265.[90] By 1929 industry in Midland County employed 43 people and produced goods worth $627,390.[91] Some of these plants were making tools and other goods for use in the oil business. Even more important by this time was the presence of oil in surrounding counties, for 147 people in Midland County were employed in this new industry.[92] As a result of the oil industry, unemployment in 1930 was virtually unknown in the county.[93]

A temporary stimulus to the town's prosperity was the building of a second railroad to Midland in 1916. Already situated on the main line of the Texas and Pacific, the town welcomed the arrival of the Midland and Northwestern, which ran to Seminole and promised future service to areas north of Midland.[94] The road was abandoned shortly after World War I, because the area it served was unable to supply enough business to permit its existence.

With the oil industry bringing more and more people to Midland, a few men who had enough vision to see the future of the town began constructing new buildings. In 1926 Dr. J. B. Thomas started the trend when he built a six-story structure that was used as a combina-

[87] *Twelfth Census of the United States, 1900: Manufactures,* II, 870.
[88] *Midland Reporter,* pp. 6–7.
[89] Texas, Department of Agriculture, *Year Book, 1909,* p. 583.
[90] *Fourteenth Census of the United States, 1920: Manufactures,* IX, 1450.
[91] *Fifteenth Census of the United States, 1930: Population,* III, Part II, 1045.
[92] *Ibid., Unemployment,* I, 995.
[93] Jo Dean Downing, comp., "The Story of Midland," p. 5, Midland County File, Bureau of Business Research, University of Texas, Austin, Texas.
[94] *Houston Chronicle,* January 3, 1954, Rotogravure Section.

tion office building and hospital. Two years later Clarence Scharbauer, having made great profits from cattle raising, began construction of a 150-room hotel.[95] In 1930 a 100-room addition to the hotel
was planned, and the Scharbauer Hotel remained the largest one in
the city.

In March 1928 T. S. Hogan, an oil operator in Montana and
Colorado, announced plans for a twelve-story office building for
Midland.[96] Although called "Hogan's Folly" by local residents, the
Petroleum Building was built to accommodate the 54 oil companies
that already had representatives in Midland in 1928.[97] Although the
buildings constructed during the late twenties were perhaps ambitious for the town at the time, the men who backed them were
accurate in their estimates of the future of Midland.

Entertainment and recreation for the residents of the community
were infrequent and usually simple. In 1898 plans were made for a
Cowboy Carnival. The event was well publicized, and 2,500 people
came to Midland and were temporarily housed in churches of the
town. The first night of the Carnival a storm blew up and a record
fourteen inches of snow fell, ending the entertainment for the
season.[98] In 1909 the philanthropy of Andrew Carnegie resulted in
the establishment of a library in the town, and in 1916 a movie
house, the Unique Theater, was offering nightly entertainment for
the nominal charge of $.05 for children and $.10 for adults.[99] With
these few exceptions, the residents of Midland had little in the way
of organized entertainment.

Midland owed its continued existence to the decision of the Texas
and Pacific Railroad to pass through it and to the fact that the
community was the county seat of Midland County. The first building
serving as headquarters for county government was a wooden structure built in 1890. In 1905 this courthouse was replaced by a three-

---

[95] *West Texas Today*, X (August, 1929), 11.
[96] *Ibid.*, IX (March, 1928).
[97] *Ibid.*
[98] Mrs. George Glass, *History of Midland*, p. 7.
[99] Texas, Department of Agriculture, *Year Book, 1909*, p. 583; and Downing,
"Story of Midland," p. 18.

story red sandstone building that was used until 1929 when it was auctioned off for $1.00.[100] At that time a modern office building was constructed for the purpose of housing county offices. The town was primarily a mercantile and service center for business of all sorts in the county.

By 1930 Midland was a small city of just over 5,000 people. Centered in an area mostly devoted to ranching, its merchants served the needs of the entire county. At that time the first impact of the oil industry was beginning to be felt, and the large hotel and the twelve-story office building attested to the economic future of the town. Perhaps more than any other community in the area considered, Midland had begun to develop into a small modern city.

Odessa, county seat of Ector County, was even smaller than neighboring Midland in 1930, but like Midland, Odessa contained a majority of the people living in the county. Ector County was a ranching section in which farming was still in its infancy at the end of this period and in which the oil industry was just beginning. One writer reported that in 1900 "Odessa was a small cowtown with two prominent saloons, an 'opry' house, a blacksmith shop, a two-by-five jail, two grocery stores, a hotel, two eating joints, a meat market, and a variety store."[101] This was probably a fairly accurate description of the small village of 381 inhabitants, for four years later J. M. Frame, the Texas and Pacific agent at Odessa wrote that "there is nothing here but stock raising, though it may be farming or granger country some day. Not much prospects for the town to grow." Indeed, at that time the town probably would have passed from existence had it not been for the railroad.[102]

Most of the business district of Odessa was completed just before the turn of the century. In 1897 a large general merchandise store was opened by B. Blankenship and Company. In the same year the brick hotel was built by J. W. Buchanan, and the Malone Lumber

[100] Glass, *History of Midland*, p. 6.

[101] Finas Wade Horton, "A History of Ector County, Texas" (Master's Thesis, University of Texas, 1950), p. 46.

[102] Velma Barrett and Hazel Oliver, *Odessa: City of Dreams, A Miracle of the Texas Prairies*, p. 106.

Company was opened for business.[103] No bank was chartered in Odessa until 1902 when the Odessa National was started, only to fail in a year.[104] In 1906 the Citizens National and the Western National were both opened, and after the Panic of 1907 the two consolidated under the name of the first.[105]

Not until the year of the Panic was a city election for municipal offices held. In that year a public power plant was also established, and electricity could be turned on two afternoons a week.[106] By 1907 the business district of Odessa had two general stores, two hotels, and the banks. The *Ector County Democrat* was the only newspaper in the town at the time, and by 1910 it had followed the lead of its predecessors, the *Odessa Weekly News,* which lasted for only one year in 1896, and the *Times,* which was published during 1904 and 1905 and then went out of business. The *Odessa Herald* managed to continue in existence for twelve years following 1910, and the *Ector County Times* began publication in 1925 and lasted to the present time, changing its name in 1948 to the *Odessa American.*[107]

A similar lack of success attended the first attempt to establish a public school system in Odessa in 1890, but the following year efforts in this direction were crowned with success. The first classes were held in a wooden structure, but in 1898 a red brick two-story building was completed by means of public subscription.[108] At that time the state superintendent of schools listed only 73 students in Ector County. Although the number rose to nearly 350 for the period 1901–1911, it fell to 188 between 1910 and 1921.[109] By the end of World War I the schools of the county, with the exception of those in Odessa, had fallen into decay because the county population was so dispersed and because finances were inadequate to attract teachers to rural areas. Private classes were held on a number of ranches

[103] Horton, "History of Ector County," p. 46.

[104] Barrett and Oliver, *Odessa,* p. 27.

[105] "Odessa, Texas, History of Odessa and Odessa's Meteorite Crater," no page, Ector County File, Bureau of Business Research, University of Texas, Austin, Texas.

[106] *Ibid.*

[107] Horton, "History of Ector County," pp. 49–51.

[108] *Ibid.,* pp. 109, 113–115.   [109] *Ibid.,* p. 113.

throughout the county, but Odessa had the only public schools. One result of the lack of educational facilities was a low rate of attendance during the entire period up to 1930.

Ector County grew rather rapidly between 1900 and 1910, the population rising from 381 to 1,178 during the decade.[110] By 1920 the number of people living in the county had fallen to 760.[111] This decline was not the result of the war drawing men away, since only 13 from the county were in the services, and few left for higher paying jobs.[112] Probably the effects of the drought of 1917 and 1918 on the only industry of the county, cattle raising, were so great that many people simply moved to other areas. There was apparently little real fear that the population movement would be a permanent thing, for in June 1920 a new two-story hotel was opened in Odessa.[113] By 1930 the population of the county was 3,958,[114] and the area was entering a period of great growth.

During the first three decades of the twentieth century the population of the six counties under consideration rose from 8,837 to 80,005,[115] an increase that was primarily the result of a natural movement of people to West Texas to take advantage of virgin agricultural land or of the oil discoveries in the area. Although the section was basically an agricultural one, a great many of these immigrants eventually became residents of the few towns in the area, for in 1930 the combined population of the county seats in the six counties was 39,010, nearly 50 per cent of the total population of the area.[116] In addition, there were probably 2,000 to 3,000 people living in smaller communities in the area.

A number of factors caused the growth of towns during these years. Although the westward movement in Texas in the early years of the century did not constitute a genuine land rush, it did have

---

[110] *Thirteenth Census of the United States, 1910: Population*, III, 782.

[111] *Fourteenth Census of the United States, 1920: Population*, I, 130.

[112] Horton, "History of Ector County," p. 69.

[113] *Big Spring Herald*, May 27, 1921.

[114] *Fifteenth Census of the United States, 1930: Population*, III, Part II, 994.

[115] *Twelfth Census of the United States, 1900: Population*, I; and *Fifteenth Census of the United States, 1930: Population*, III, Part II.

[116] *Fifteenth Census of the United States, 1930: Population*, III, Part II.

some characteristics of one since many people were unprepared, financially or by previous training, to take advantage of the supposed profits of farming in West Texas. A great many of them subsequently found that they were unable to continue as farmers and either moved to another section or went into the towns to find work.

Another factor causing movement into towns was the uncertainty of weather conditions in West Texas. A case in point was the severe drought of 1917–1918 which forced some farmers and ranchers to leave their land. Between 1910 and 1920 a great deal of West Texas land was taken out of cultivation. Furthermore, the land in the area simply could not support a large rural population; therefore, the urban population was large in proportion to the rural for an agricultural section.

Towns already established when the Texas and Pacific reached the area in 1881–1882, and towns at which depots were set up by the railroad, were naturally the first to develop. The presence of the railroad and of an adequate supply of water made it almost inevitable that these early communities would become important in West Texas. The need for transportation facilities for shipment of farm and ranch produce was imperative in the region, and without a sufficient amount of water, no community could exist for long. With the exception of Snyder and Lamesa, each of the county seats was located on the Texas and Pacific, and these two towns later got railroad connections. Each of the towns had a water supply available either in the form of a ground-water source or as surface water.

Although agriculture was the dominant interest of the people in this area throughout the period before 1930, and although the total value of farm production in the six counties rose from $907,333 in 1900 to $11,114,405 by 1930,[117] other businesses and industries were beginning to dominate the economy. Farming and ranching still employed more workers in these six counties than any other single industry,[118] but business and industry combined not only

---

[117] *Twelfth Census of the United States, 1900: Agriculture,* I.

[118] About 40 per cent of the people gainfully employed in the six counties were in agricultural pursuits. The nearest occupations to agriculture in order of

accounted for a larger number of workers but also were rapidly expanding while agriculture remained static. Manufacturing, only starting at the turn of the century, produced goods valued at $186,131 in 1900.[119] By 1929 industry was becoming increasingly important, and in that year the value of manufactured goods in the area reached more than $16,000,000.[120] Both relatively and absolutely industry had grown more rapidly than farming. Although many of the industries processed agricultural products, manufactures allied with mineral products were also growing quickly in number and size.

The greatest period of growth for the towns of the area occurred between 1900 and 1910. Businessmen were able to purchase land at low prices, and many of the merchants and professional men in the towns also became owners of ranches or farms during this period. Eventually a demand for land came with the influx of people, and these landowners realized great profits on their investments. A similar situation developed when oil was first discovered. Those on the scene who had money available were the ones who reaped the benefits from the new industry.

In 1930 one period of development in central West Texas was at an end and another was about to begin. Always an agricultural area, these counties relied almost entirely on the farmers and ranchers for trade and income. The discovery of oil in Mitchell County in 1920 ended a long-standing conviction on the part of geologists that West Texas would never be an oil-producing area and inaugurated a widespread search for petroleum that affected every county in the region. In 1930 the oil industry was just beginning and had hardly made an impression on the economy of the area; within a decade it was to be the most important factor in that economy.

---

size were transportation and communication, building industries, oil and gas, and manufacturing and industry (*ibid., Occupations,* III, Part II).

[119] *Ibid., Manufactures,* II.
[120] *Fifteenth Census of the United States, 1930: Manufactures,* III.

CHAPTER SIX

THE OIL INDUSTRY IN WEST TEXAS BEFORE 1930

APPROXIMATELY TWO MILLION years ago, in the latter part of the Paleozoic Era called the Permian period, many of the oil-bearing formations of West Texas were deposited.[1] In this period, mountain ranges were elevated, saline deposits were formed, continents were uplifted and enlarged, and shallow seas gradually subsided from large land areas that they had covered.[2] In the present United States rocks of Permian age were exposed in three sections: (1) the northern Appalachian area; (2) the mid-continent region, including West Texas and eastern New Mexico; and (3) widely scattered areas in the western part of the continent.[3] By far the largest area of surface outcrops was exposed in the mid-continent region. In early Permian time marine conditions probably existed over all of western Texas and eastern New Mexico. Although the main body of the Permian sea lay to the southwest of this area, an arm covered the

---

[1] Charles Schuchert and Carl O. Dunbar, *Outlines of Historical Geology*, p. 14. The name Permian came from the province of Perm in northeastern Russia where the first Permian formations were identified by the British geologist, Murchison, in 1841 (Raymond G. Moore, *Historical Geology*, p. 316).

[2] Moore, *Historical Geology*, p. 316, and Schuchert and Dunbar, *Outlines of Historical Geology*, p. 16.

[3] Moore, *Historical Geology*, p. 317.

region and extended into West-Central Oklahoma and Kansas,[4] forming what was later called the Permian Basin.

In the southern Llano Estacado and Trans-Pecos regions of Texas, marine formations of limestone and some shale and sandstone accumulated along the shores of this sea, and a little later red beds were deposited.[5] These formations possessed a porosity capable of acting as a trap for petroleum. Toward the close of the Permian epoch the climate became more humid, and as land masses rose, rivers carried terrestrial and near-shore sediments of red muds and sand that were dropped by the streams rushing into the sea and were deposited along the shores.[6] These sediments covered and carried with them the organic, petroleum-forming life of the area, and thus the Permian Basin with its untold riches was formed and awaited man's coming.

Although settlement of the part of West Texas that overlay the Permian Basin did not take place until after the Civil War, some minor work on the geology of the area already had been done. One of the first works dealing with the geology of Texas was published in 1849 in Bonn, Germany, by Ferdinand Roemer under the title, "Texas, With Observations on Its Natural History and Geology."[7] The western part of the state was included in a topographical map of Texas which accompanied the work. More important than this publication were a number of exploratory expeditions crossing West Texas in the latter half of the nineteenth century. Some of these groups were accompanied by scientists, and notes taken by these men contained the earliest observations of the geology and geography of the Permian Basin.

George G. Shumard, geologist for the 1852 expedition that Randolph B. Marcy made along the Red River, placed the strata of the Llano Estacado in the Cretaceous period.[8] The following year Jules

[4] H. W. Hoots, *Geology of a Part of Western Texas and Southeastern New Mexico: With a Special Reference to Salt and Potash*, p. 122.

[5] *Ibid.*; and Moore, *Historical Geology*, p. 330.

[6] Hoots, *Geology of a Part of Western Texas*, p. 122.

[7] S. B. Buckley, *First Annual Report of the Geological and Agricultural Survey of Texas*, p. 6.

[8] Randolph B. Marcy, *Exploration of the Red River of Louisiana in the Year 1852*, pp. 156–157.

Marcou, a government geologist, traveled through the northern part of the Texas plains and concluded that the rocks he discovered were of Jurassic age.[9] In 1853 and 1854 C. C. Parry and Arthur Schott, scientists connected with the boundary survey made by Major W. H. Emory, made observations and collected fossils, which were later studied and reported on by James Hall and T. A. Conrad for the federal government. Fossils collected by members of the railroad survey group led by Captain John Pope in 1853 were subjected to a preliminary analysis by Jules Marcou, and later a more complete study was completed by W. P. Blake, who found the outcrops along the route from Big Spring to the Pecos River to be Cretaceous and Tertiary in age.[10]

In 1858 the Texas legislature established a geological and agricultural survey, but almost no work was done in the western part of the state.[11] Between 1860 and 1888 only one paper, an article published by J. P. Kimball in 1869, dealt directly with the geology of West Texas.[12] In 1888 the state geological survey was re-established, and after that date systematic work was accomplished by both Texas and the federal government.

In the first report of progress made by Edwin T. Dumble, geologist for the Texas Geological and Mineralogical Survey, the presence of gas in wells drilled for water or coal was reported in West Texas.[13] Although this was the only mention of possible indications of the presence of petroleum in the area, a considerable amount of valuable

[9] Hoots, *Geology of a Part of Western Texas*, p. 57.

[10] George Burr Richardson, *Report of a Reconnaissance in Trans-Pecos Texas, North of the Texas and Pacific Railway*, p. 13.

[11] The legislature ordered an agricultural and geological survey of the state to be made by a state geologist, an assistant state geologist, and a chemist. Dr. Benjamin F. Shumard was appointed state geologist and in turn designated his brother, Dr. George G. Shumard, as his assistant, and Dr. Riddell as chemist (Buckley, *Geological and Agricultural Survey of Texas*, p. 7).

[12] Richardson, *Report of a Reconnaissance*, p. 16.

[13] Although several such indications of the presence of petroleum had been reported, no efforts had been made to locate oil (Edwin T. Dumble, *First Report of Progress of the Geological and Mineralogical Survey of Texas*, pp. 18, 23).

geological work was done during the last decade of the nineteenth century.

A paper by W. F. Cummins and Dr. Otto Lerch appearing in *American Geology* in 1890 gave a summary of information on the Texas Permian up to that time.[14] Charles A. White made a geological trip across West Texas in 1891 and in a United States Geological Survey Bulletin showed the Permian age of some of the strata studied in the region.[15] The first detailed work dealing with the stratigraphy of parts of the Permian Basin was that of Robert Taff in 1891 and 1892, and in 1893 R. S. Tarr discussed the physical geography of the same section.[16] Robert T. Hill applied the term Permian to formations in the Trans-Pecos region of Texas in an 1887 article, and in 1900 he compiled all available data on the physical geography of this and other areas.[17] Because of the growing interest in geology, a small store of information concerning the formations of the Permian Basin had been accumulated from a variety of sources by the turn of the century.

Until 1900 petroleum was not of major importance to many geologists. Surveys were generally made in order to study the strata and physical geology of a region or to view the area for possible evidences of coal or other minerals. Mention of petroleum in papers dealing with West Texas consisted mainly of references to oil seeps, traces of oil and gas in water wells, and asphalt or tar deposits. After the discovery of the fabulous Spindletop well at Beaumont in 1901, geologists became more interested in locating oil-bearing formations, and the Permian area of Texas was studied in the hope of finding oil.

[14] The paper covered Tom Green, Coke, and Irion counties in West Texas. The authors divided Permian strata into three formations, Wichita, Clear Fork, and Double Mountain (Hoots, *Geology of a Part of Western Texas*, p. 57; and W. P. Bently, *The Geology of Coke County*, p. 13).

[15] Charles A. White, *The Texas Permian and Its Mesozoic Types of Fossils*, p. 8.

[16] Hoots, *Geology of a Part of Western Texas*, p. 58.

[17] Robert T. Hill, *The Present Condition of Knowledge of the Geology of Texas*, p. 7.

William Battle Phillips became director of the University of Texas Mineral Survey in 1901, and under his direction a number of bulletins on the geology of West Texas were published. The federal government was also carrying on work in the Permian area in 1901, and in a United States publication George I. Adams wrote of various oil seepages in West Texas.[18] During the early years of the twentieth century a number of geological expeditions traveled through West Texas, and by the end of World War I geologists felt that they had exhausted the possibilities of the area as far as the discovery of oil was concerned.

Although the work done before 1920 greatly increased the knowledge of scientists concerning the formations beneath the arid soil of West Texas, the consensus of the experts was that there could be little hope of finding petroleum in commercial quantities in the region. The sum of the information was negative, and most of the reports concluded that the Permian strata were incapable of forming the necessary traps to catch oil. To the geologist's eye there were no indications of the vast wealth in oil which the Permian Basin was to yield.

Despite the pessimism of geologists, wells were drilled by wildcatters in various parts of the Permian Basin.[19] Traces of oil and gas were found in some of the wells, and there were also promising surface indications of the possible occurrence of petroleum in West Texas, but neither of these factors led to the first commercial oil

[18] George I. Adams, *Oil and Gas Fields of the Western Interior and Northern Texas Coal Measures and of the Upper Cretaceous and Tertiary of the Western Gulf Coast*, p. 29.

[19] The use of immense quantities of oil in World War I, the increasing importance of the automobile, and the use of oil as a fuel by many navies showed the value of oil and spurred the search for it. By 1901, attempts to find oil had been made in the Pecos Valley (*Dallas Morning News*, March 2 and April 24, 1901). Before 1920 wells were drilled in other parts of West Texas. (See G. B. Richardson, "Salt, Gypsum, and Petroleum in Trans-Pecos Texas," *Contributions to Economic Geology in 1904*, p. 581; *Mineral Resources of the United States*, 1901, p. 531, and 1913; Part II: Non-Metals, p. 1046; Samuel W. Tait, *The Wildcatters, An Informal History of Oil Hunting in America*, p. 130; G. B. Richardson, "Petroleum Near Dayton, New Mexico," *Contributions to Economic Geology in 1912*, p. 136; and R. A. Liddle, *The Marathon Fold and Its Influence on Petroleum Accumulation*, p. 13.)

discovery in the area. Rather it was a matter of chance; the drilling of wildcats based on hope was responsible for opening the Permian Basin to oil production.

In 1919 Steve Owens, general field manager for the Underwriters Producing Company, was obligated to drill a wildcat on leases north of Westbrook in Mitchell County.[20] A dry hole was put down during the year, and in 1920 the company prepared to begin a second test. On February 8, 1920, the well was spudded in using a cable tool rig, and at 500 feet the bit struck the first oil found in commercial quantities in the Permian Basin. This was the first well to be produced from Permian age strata, previously considered a poor prospect. Since the oil found had a high salt content, this sand was cased off and the well continued to 2,489 feet where it was completed on March 5, 1921 as a ten-barrel producer.[21]

When news of the discovery reached Colorado City, the headlines of the local paper reported, "Oil in Mitchell County . . . the Golden Flood Is Struck."[22] Although the editor was unduly optimistic concerning the future of oil in the county, since the Westbrook field was never a major producer, he had unknowingly predicted the future of West Texas. The fact that oil in commercial quantities could be found in the area acted as a catalyst, setting off a chain reaction of oil exploration throughout the Permian Basin.

A second field in Mitchell County was opened in 1925, the Iatan-East Howard field, located about fifteen miles east of Big Spring.[23]

[20] *Drill Bit*, II (October, 1954), 58; and Watt Collier, interview with C. C. Rister, Colorado City, Texas, December 28, 1948.

[21] American Association of Petroleum Geologists, *Structure of Typical American Oil Fields*, I, 284.

[22] *Colorado City* (Texas) *Record*, August 25, 1939; and the *Texas Spur and Dickens Item*, July 9, 1920. The best well in the field was the third test put down, Underwriters Company number 2 Morrison, completed in 1921 at 2,972 feet in what was called the Morrison sand, occurring near the base of the Clear Fork. The 2,400-foot pay in the discovery well was near the Double Mountain–Clear Fork contact. Within two years of the discovery, the holdings of the Underwriters Company were purchased by a major company, the California Company, now Standard Oil of Texas (American Association of Petroleum Geologists, *Structure of Typical American Oil Fields*, I, 284–287).

[23] Carl Coke Rister, *Oil! Titan of the Southwest*, p. 286.

By 1930 this field was extended into Howard County where the greater part of the pool was eventually determined. Before this development, oil fever had already resulted in a search for oil in Howard County. Between 1919 and 1921 a boom was started as a result of the drilling in Mitchell County. This was a boom rather than a development because unscrupulous speculators were responsible for it, and no oil was actually found.

The Big Spring Production Company was formed to sink a test well on the Quinn Ranch, west of Big Spring. In January 1921, the *Big Spring Herald* reported that 30 citizens of the town had each donated $52.00 so that the crew might be paid and said that others would have to contribute if the well were to be completed.[24] In order to secure more investors in the project, S. E. J. Cox, the promoter

To CORRECT ERRORS ON PAGE 102
THE CITY MOVES WEST

S. E. J. Cox was not associated with the Big Spring Production Company, but was rather president of the General Oil Company which began operations in the Big Spring area in 1919. The General Oil Company completed a number of producing wells in Howard County.

later.

During the first days of November 1925 Fred Hyer was drilling a wildcat test on land leased from H. R. Clay in Howard County, not far from the Glasscock County line.[28] On February 26, 1926, the *Oil and Gas Journal* reported that "Western Texas has another wildcat well that is making a very interesting showing as a producer . . .

[24] *Big Spring* (Texas) *Herald*, January 7, 1921.
[25] *Big Spring* (Texas) *Daily Herald*, April 26, 1936.
[26] *Big Spring Herald*, February 11, 1921, February 25, 1921, and April 1, 1921.
[27] *Ibid.*, January 28, 1921.
[28] *Oil and Gas Journal*, XXIV (November 26, 1925), 28.

the number 1 Clay of Fred Hyer in the southeastern part of Howard County."[29] Initial reports indicated that the well would probably produce about 50 barrels from the 1,546–1,566-foot sand.[30] This well was the discovery location of the Howard-Glasscock pool, the first oil field in Howard County. The multireservoir pool was a long and narrow S-shaped anticline extending into Glasscock County although the majority of the production was located in Howard County.[31]

The discovery of oil in Howard County initiated a drilling campaign that lasted throughout the late twenties and resulted in the discovery of several oil fields in the county. In the early spring of 1926 the *Big Spring Herald* followed with interest developments of the well being drilled by Steve Owens and S. A. Sloan, independent operators from Colorado City.[32] This test, located on the Chalk Ranch in the extreme southeast corner of the county, was completed in April 1926, as a 40-barrel producer from the 1,577-foot pay.[33] Owens and Sloan held 1,390 acres under lease in the immediate vicinity of the well.

Wildcatting activity proved so successful in West Texas in 1926 that seven new pools were discovered and the same number of counties were proved for production. The *Mineral Resources of the United States* for that year reported that because of these successes, "West Texas is regarded as the greatest future source of domestic supply" of oil.[34] Activity in Howard County helped confirm this prediction. In May 1926 the Snyder field in southeast Howard County was opened with the completion of the discovery well, Choate and Henshaw's number 1 M. H. McDaniel in the Glorietta formation of Permian age.[35] A year later the small Moore field was discovered by

[29] *Ibid.*, XXIV (February 26, 1926), 30.
[30] The largest leaseholders were Humble and Marland oil companies. It was the usual case for majors or large independents to control acreage near important discoveries (*ibid.*).
[31] *Mineral Resources of the United States*, 1929, Part II: Non-Metals, p. 459.
[32] *Big Spring Herald*, February 1 to April 23, 1926.
[33] *Oil and Gas Journal*, XXIV (April 29, 1926), 39.
[34] *Mineral Resources of the United States*, 1926, Part II: Non-Metals, p. 358.
[35] George H. Fancher, *et al.*, *The Oil Resources of Texas*, p. 289.

Marland Oil Company *et al* number 1 J. B. Harding, and in June 1930 the Iatan-East Howard field, about fifteen miles east of Big Spring, was extended into Howard County.[36]

Although the successful drilling in Mitchell and Howard counties stimulated similar activity in neighboring areas, most of them were not so fortunate in locating production. In Nolan County no oil was found, but the county did receive some benefit from the petroleum industry because two refineries were constructed at Sweetwater during this period. The Sweetwater Refining Company was a local venture and was forced to shut down during 1926, but the Gulf Sweetwater Refinery, built in 1929, continued to operate until 1954.[37]

In Scurry County drillers were a little more successful, and in December 1923 the discovery well in the Sharon Ridge field was brought in as a twenty-five–barrel producer from the San Andres formation.[38] This field, about ten miles from Snyder, was the only one in the county until 1948 and was extended into Mitchell County in 1940. Drilling on a limited scale continued in the county, but with no success.

The most important oil production in the area under consideration was the result of wildcats drilled in Ector County. The first oil and gas lease on record in the county was made in 1919 between G. F. Cowden and E. F. Cowden, who leased land to W. R. Chancellor for five years for the sum of $1,280.[39] A total of 43 leases were made in 1919, and two years later 60,000 acres of land near Odessa had been leased in order to determine the value of potash and oil deposits in the area.[40] Early in the twenties a well was put down on the present site of Odessa by the Farmer's Oil Company. This organization suffered the fate of many companies organized during a period of great expectations, and the well was abandoned at 1,000 feet because

[36] *Ibid.*; and *Oil and Gas Journal*, XXV (May 12, 1927), 39.

[37] *Oil and Gas Journal*, XXIV (January 14, 1926), 38; and *Drill Bit*, II (November, 1954), 55.

[38] *Abilene* (Texas) *Reporter*, December 18, 1923.

[39] Finas Wade Horton, "A History of Ector County, Texas," (Master's Thesis, University of Texas, 1950), p. 88.

[40] *Big Spring Herald*, August 5, 1921.

of lack of funds.[41] The company was dissolved shortly afterward. Even though no oil had been found, the town of Odessa received some business from discoveries in Crane County since the Ector County seat was the nearest railroad shipping point.

The first oil actually discovered in the county was on the W. E. Connell Ranch, about fifteen miles west of Odessa, in the fall of 1926.[42] The first well drilled on this location was eventually abandoned because of the limited production, and a second wildcat was located three miles east of the Connell test. This well was drilled by W. A. Black for Robert Penn and was completed in October 1929.[43] The Penn-Well field included both the Connell discovery and the Penn extension. *Mineral Resources of the United States* reported the field as one of the most important discovered in 1929.[44] The following year the Penn-Well field was a key factor in Texas oil production because the pool yielded more than 3,000,000 barrels of oil during 1930.[45]

The Connell discovery stimulated extensive exploration in Ector County, and in September 1930 a new pool was opened eighteen miles northwest of Odessa. The North Cowden field was discovered with the completion of Southern Crude Purchasing Company's number 1 Cowden.[46] Four different producing zones were located in this well, which opened a second major field in Ector County.[47]

The Cowden wildcat created a problem concerning the storage of oil. Five 500-barrel tanks were erected immediately, and a 10,000-barrel storage tank was ordered, but at the time of discovery no pipeline facilities were available, and there was some conjecture as to whether or not a pipeline would be built.[48] Eventually, as other

[41] Horton, "History of Ector County," p. 88.
[42] *Ibid.*; and *Oil and Gas Journal*, XXVI (October 6, 1929), 41.
[43] *Sweetwater* (Texas) *Reporter*, October 17, 1929.
[44] *Mineral Resources of the United States*, 1929, Part II: Non-Metals, p. 460.
[45] *Ibid.*, 1930, Part II: Non-Metals, p. 814.
[46] Fancher, *Oil Resources*, p. 282.
[47] The field produced from four separate zones of the Grayburg limestone of the Guadalupe series of formations (*ibid.*).
[48] The number 1 Cowden was estimated at between 300 and 500 barrels per day of 29.8 degree gravity oil. The pay was picked up at 4,130 feet, filling the

wells were completed, and it was realized that a major field had been uncovered, transportation facilities were constructed to the area.

The North Cowden field and other wildcat discoveries in West Texas also created problems for oil operators and for the Railroad Commission of Texas, which had administrative control of oil production. These new oil discoveries appeared at the same time that oilmen in the state were engrossed in curtailing production in the various active areas to coincide with the general proration plan of Texas.[49] The pools opened in the Permian Basin brought additional oil into consideration in the overall planning.

The decade of the twenties proved a profitable one for the people on the arid lands of West Texas, for during these years a tremendous new industry, one whose future was then unimaginable, was opened up in the area. By 1927 the *Mineral Resources of the United States* reported that the events of that year proved that the optimistic predictions of 1926 had been surpassed. Total production of the West Texas district for 1927 was 51,538,000 barrels as compared with 14,758,000 barrels the preceding year.[50] This record was all the more remarkable because a majority of the wells were either shut down or pinched in during parts of the year and consequently produced only a portion of their potential.

The leasing and wildcatting campaign that resulted from discoveries in the area continued in 1927, and a few new fields were located. During that year one of the most important discoveries was that of deep lime production in the Chalk field in Howard County, the first discovery of that kind on the east side of the Permian Basin.[51] Beside the location of new fields, other activities in the area included the completion of several new trunk pipelines from West Texas to the Gulf Coast, indicating the importance of the region as a producer.[52]

---

hole with oil. Southern Crude had about 5,000 acres under lease near the well (*Oil and Gas Journal,* XXIX [September 11, 1930], 69, and [September 18, 1930], 71).

[49] *Ibid.,* XXIX (September 11, 1930), 69.

[50] *Mineral Resources of the United States,* 1927, Part II: Non-Metals, p. 206.

[51] *Ibid.,* p. 206.

[52] A tank-building program begun earlier was temporarily curtailed because

By 1928 total production of West Texas oil fields reached 123,540,000 barrels of oil, nearly half of the total output for the state in that year.[53] This production from an area that did not have a single producing well in 1920 severely taxed the transportation facilities of the region, and a huge tank-building program was necessary. The expanding activities of the petroleum industry and the construction of refineries in West Texas strengthened the market, and crude prices quoted in contracts gradually increased during 1928.[54]

Interest in finding new oil fields in the Permian Basin caused a wildcatting campaign during the twenties which materially improved the economic future of West Texas. By 1930 there were more than 800 producing wells in the area being considered.[55] Oil-connected industries were also located in the region and brought additional revenue to the counties concerned. Six refineries had been built in Sweetwater, Midland, and Big Spring, and natural gasoline plants were utilizing gas from the fields in the Permian Basin.[56]

The towns in West Texas were affected by the development of the oil industry. The discovery of oil brought on a period of speculation and exploration which, although not always successful, helped stimulate business of all sorts in the area. There was an influx of population which was mostly temporary, but a few of the people who moved to new areas of oil development always became permanent residents. It was during these years that many town improvements were carried out, for most of the towns obtained natural gas for the first time, and some of them paved their streets.[57] Buildings to accommodate offices of oil companies were constructed in Midland

---

of the corrosive action of sulphur in some of the West Texas crudes. New tanks had to be developed for the storage of this oil (*ibid.*).

[53] *Mineral Resources of the United States,* 1928, Part II: Non-Metals, p. 646.

[54] *Ibid.,* pp. 647–648.

[55] *Oil and Gas Journal,* XXIX (September 18, 1930), 71.

[56] *Ibid.,* XXIX (September 11, 1930), 73. As early as 1928 Howard, Reagan, and Mitchell counties produced 9,827,000 gallons of gasoline valued at $597,000 (*Mineral Resources of the United States,* 1928, Part II: Non-Metals, p. 212).

[57] *Big Spring Daily Herald,* April 26, 1936.

and Big Spring. The total effect of the discovery of oil by 1930 was partially to replace decreasing income from agricultural production and to prepare the area for the years of the depression.

Ten years after the oil boom in West Texas started, it as suddenly stopped, but only temporarily. The discovery of prolific oil fields in East Texas in 1930 brought about an almost wholesale removal of oilmen, drilling crews, and equipment, including refineries, tanks, and drilling rigs, from the Permian Basin fields.[58] As a result, drilling activity was curtailed, and only 170 wells were drilled in 1930 as compared with 495 the preceding year.[59] Although some exploration continued and a few new fields were discovered in West Texas, the real oil interest in Texas was transferred to the eastern part of the state.

The record of the oil industry in West Texas during the twenties, though impressive, was but a forerunner of subsequent developments, however. A great deal of the work done in this decade was unprofessional in that luck and hunches played almost as great a part in the discoveries as did science. In contrast, the great boom of the forties was to be the result of information already gathered, the experience of the past, and the technological and scientific developments of the intervening years.

[58] *Mineral Resources of the United States*, 1931, Part II: Non-Metals, pp. 585–586.
[59] *Ibid.*, p. 586.

CHAPTER SEVEN

THE WEST TEXAS OIL INDUSTRY COMES OF AGE

THE SHIFT IN INTEREST of the oil fraternity from West to East Texas in 1930 and 1931 did not mean the end of exploratory activities in the Permian Basin. Although the movement out of West Texas was a large-scale one, it was not in any sense a permanent relocation of activities. During the thirties a great deal of the exploration in the counties under consideration was connected with the extension of fields already discovered to determine their limits. Representative of this type of drilling were wells in the Iatan–East Howard and the Howard-Glasscock pools. Another kind of test conducted in these years was an Ordovician test planned for Mitchell County in 1932 in an attempt to locate a deeper pay zone in the old Westbrook field.[1]

Some wildcat wells were also put down in the hope of finding new fields. By far the most promising area was in Ector County where the Cowden and Penn-Well pools had proven so productive, and it was here that much of the activity of the thirties took place. The expectations of oilmen bore fruit in November 1932, when the Harrison, Turner, *et al* number 1 Addis was completed as the discovery well of the South Cowden field.[2] On December 1 it was reported that the

[1] *Oil and Gas Journal,* XXXI (December 1, 1932), 41.
[2] This was also called the Addis field (George H. Fancher, ed., *The Oil Resources of Texas,* p. 282).

well would be at least a 100-barrel a day producer, and the test was still being drilled at 3,800 feet in the hope of locating an even bigger pay. The discovery was heralded as the first important one in the two years since attention was focused on East Texas. That additional drilling would follow was assured since both Stanolind Oil and Gas and Humble Oil and Refining held several adjoining and surrounding sections.[3]

In the middle of December the Addis well was flowing 200 barrels.[4] Drilling was continued until early in 1933. The South Cowden field was only five miles from Odessa and was to create new business for that community. By December 22 a four-inch pipeline was being constructed to take oil from the well to loading racks on the Texas and Pacific Railroad, only one and one-half miles south of the well, from which petroleum would be carried to the Howard County refinery at Big Spring.[5]

In 1933 the search for oil continued, spurred on by the successful completion of the Addis well, and another important field was discovered in Ector County. Phillips Petroleum Company, which had leased land from E. F. Cowden, spudded in the number 1 C. F. Cowden in December of that year.[6] This discovery well of the Harper field, while still drilling, was thought to be a 100- to 150-barrel producer, and when completed proved to be even better than the estimate. Humble Pipe Line Company, which had recently laid a line from the Penn-Well fields to the North and South Cowden pools, prepared to lay a four-inch connecting line to the new Harper field.[7] In addition to the Humble facilities, both Magnolia Pipe Line and Gulf Pipe Line had carriers within a few miles of the field.[8]

Development of the area surrounding the discovery well was relatively slow as there was little activity in West Texas generally. The entire field comprised about 3,800 acres in the approximate center

[3] *Oil and Gas Journal,* XXXI (December 1, 1932), 41.
[4] *Ibid.,* XXXI (December 8, 1932), 36.
[5] *Ibid.,* XXXI (December 22, 1932), 43.
[6] Fancher, *Oil Resources,* 282.
[7] *San Angelo* (Texas) *Standard-Times,* October 5, 1933.
[8] *Oil and Gas Journal,* XXXII (October 12, 1933), 59.

of the Central Basin Platform. The largest development of the field took place in 1938, when 134 wells were put down. This was also the year of greatest production, when 2,735,074 barrels of oil were pumped. By 1952 there were 186 wells in the field, and at the end of 1954 the cumulative production was 12,046,091 barrels.[9]

The important Goldsmith field in Ector County was located fifteen miles northwest of Odessa, centering about the Goldsmith townsite.[10] A well drilled in that area in 1930 had several small shows of oil, and two other tests had produced a considerable amount of gas, condensate, and some oil in 1934.[11] In 1935 Gulf Oil Corporation reopened the area with the completion of the number 1 Goldsmith in June, producing from the San Andres limestone.[12] The Goldsmith well flowed 854 barrels the first eighteen hours through two-inch casing.[13] The importance of the discovery caused the Gulf Pipe Line Company to extend a seventeen-mile line from its station in the Penn-Well field early in July.[14]

The new fields that were added to the previous discoveries in Ector County during the mid-thirties created employment and industry for the county during the depression years. By 1937 there were 562 wells in the county, and daily average production was 23,200 barrels.[15] The fields located in these years were not the last for the county, for in 1944 the TXL field, only four miles from Goldsmith, was brought in, the discovery well producing from Devonian formations. The field encompassed the largest producing area in Devonian strata found in West Texas and also produced from a number of other formations.[16] The TXL pool contained 16,440

[9] Frank A. Herald, ed., *Occurrence of Oil and Gas in West Texas*, p. 137.
[10] The discovery of oil on the Goldsmith Ranch caused the small town of Goldsmith to mushroom temporarily in 1937 to a population of 6,000 (Finas Wade Horton, "A History of Ector County, Texas" [Master's Thesis, University of Texas, 1950], pp. 55–57).
[11] Fancher, *Oil Resources*, 282.
[12] *Oil and Gas Journal*, XXXIV (June 6, 1934), 60.
[13] *Odessa* (Texas) *American*, July 4, 1935.
[14] *Oil and Gas Journal*, XXXIV (July 25, 1935), 122.
[15] *Ibid.*, XXXVI (August 26, 1937), 87.
[16] Fancher, *Oil Resources*, p. 282.

acres and at the end of 1953 had 460 producing wells. At that time yearly production was 11,291,718 barrels, cumulative production was almost 117,000,000 barrels, and in addition, 29,862,333 million cubic feet of gas was being taken from the field each year.[17]

With the completion of Shell and Stanolind's number 1 T. P. Land-TXL, the discovery well in the prolific TXL field, the major oil formations in Ector County had been discovered. During World War II drilling continued despite curtailment of supplies, and the wartime demand for oil brought a period of prosperity to the area. In 1945 there were 2,949 producing wells in the county, and the following year 3,015 wells yielded 35,550,310 barrels of petroleum.[18] Oil had been discovered in almost every part of the county, and by the end of 1948 the twenty-three–year oil-production total had reached 354,384,987 barrels.[19]

The search for oil did not stop after all the major fields had been located. In 1948 Cities Service Company drilled a test near the South Cowden field to the San Andres, plugged back to test the Grayburg lime, and reported the well flowing 264 barrels of oil a day.[20] Two years later plans were made to drill more than 100 wells on the southwest flank of the Goldsmith field to the 5,600-foot pay of the Clear Fork.[21] This activity was the result of important extensions of the field by wells drilled by Ed C. Lawson and Forrest Oil Corporation.

By 1952 the phenomenal development of the oil industry in Ector County had resulted in 166,120 acres of proven productivity with a total production up to that time of 521,373,119 barrels of oil.[22] At the time the county claimed the distinction of being the biggest oil-producing county in West Texas with over 65,000,000 barrels during the year.[23] Under the proration plan of Texas, Ector County was assured many years of prosperous activity since the estimated re-

[17] Herald, *Occurrence of Oil and Gas*, p. 368.
[18] *West Texas Today* (August, 1947), p. 6.
[19] *Dallas Morning News*, October 23, 1949.
[20] *Oil and Gas Journal*, XLVII (August 26, 1948), 187.
[21] *World Oil*, CXXX (February 15, 1950), 63.
[22] *Oil and Gas Journal*, L (January 7, 1952), 120.
[23] *Drill Bit*, I (April, 1953), 11.

serves of the county's fields were 1,671,371,289 barrels of oil.[24]

Although Ector County led the development of the oil industry in West Texas during much of the period between 1930 and 1954, activity was taking place in other parts of the Permian Basin. In Howard County exploration during the thirties took the form of further extensions of already discovered fields, and it was not until 1948 that a new pool was located in the county. In January of that year Seaboard Oil Company's number 1 Mildred M. Jones was completed as the discovery well in the Vealmoor field.[25] The Vealmoor was especially important since its production was from a limestone reef in the Canyon series, and it focused attention on the potential productivity of this formation in West Texas.

Other activity in Howard County concerned efforts to increase production of older fields. Beginning in 1947 the injection of salt water into the Howard-Glasscock field was started in the hope of realizing more profit from the pool.[26] A second water-flooding project in the field was begun in 1952 by Sunray Oil Corporation, and it was predicted that during 1954 the wells in the operation would surpass the previous peak in daily production of 5,000 barrels set in 1929.[27] Although Howard County was a minor oil producer when compared to some of the other counties in the Permian Basin, by 1952 total production since the first discovery of oil was 190,849,937 barrels. The reserves of the 31,830 proven productive acres were estimated at almost 500,000,000 barrels.[28]

Of the counties under consideration, Nolan County had the smallest amount of production, and oil in the county was discovered much later than in the rest of the region. As late as 1951 there was only one small producing well in Nolan County, but two years later there were 121 producing wells in the 22 pools discovered by that

[24] Fancher, *Oil Resources,* p. 282.

[25] *Ibid.* By July a fourth well in the field was nearing completion (*Oil and Gas Journal,* XLVII [July 29, 1948], 156).

[26] Fancher, *Oil Resources,* p. 282.

[27] When Sunray took over the Dora Roberts lease in 1943, daily production was only 1,300 barrels. By 1953 it had been raised to 4,500 barrels (*Drill Bit,* I [May, 1953], 17).

[28] Fancher, *Oil Resources,* p. 289.

HUNT LIBRARY
CARNEGIE-MELLON UNIVERSITY

time, and 27 rigs were in operation.[29] The leading field in production in the county was the North Dora pool, and in 1954 Sohio Petroleum Company made arrangements to purchase oil from the field and was preparing to construct a four-inch pipeline to the wells.[30] The importance of the Nolan County discoveries was indicated by the purchase in 1954 by British-American Oil Company of a 160-acre lease for $500 an acre.[31] The oil boom, though late in starting, was important for Nolan County.

For twenty-five years following the discovery of the Sharon Ridge pool in Scurry County, no other field was found in the county. Wells continued to be drilled in the Sharon Ridge area, and in 1940 this field was extended into Mitchell County, but there was little hope that bonanza production would ever be found. In 1938 Gulf Oil Corporation was drilling a well in Scurry County in which was encountered a limestone buildup 1,340 feet in thickness.[32] After five months of perforating, acidizing, and testing various zones of the reef, the well was abandoned in March 1939.[33] Six years later Lion Oil Company drilled a test on the McLaughlin Ranch in the hope of finding oil in the Permian beds from which the Sharon Ridge and Westbrook fields produced.[34] Failing to discover any production, the well was abandoned in 1945. Both the Gulf and Lion companies had barely missed discovering one of the most prolific fields in the United States.

The discovery well that actually started the widespread search for oil in Scurry County was drilled by Humble Oil and Refining and

---

[29] *Fort Worth Star-Telegram*, September 27, 1953.

[30] Sohio was planning to use 23 miles of ten-inch line that was leased from Gulf Pipe Line. Gulf had ceased operation of the line in 1954 (*Drill Bit*, II [May, 1954], 44).

[31] Texas Pacific Land Trust, which owned the land, was also to keep a 50 per cent royalty, which was extremely high (*ibid.*, p. 39).

[32] *World Oil*, CXXX (April, 1950), 40–41. The limestone reef was first discovered in the Big Lake pool in Reagan County in 1929. New interest was stimulated in the formation after it was discovered in the Vealmoor field, Howard County, in 1948 (*ibid.*, CXXXI [September 4, 1950], 73).

[33] *Ibid.*, CXXX (April, 1950), 40.

[34] *World Petroleum*, XXI (April, 1950), 36.

Sun Oil as the number 1 Emil Schattel and was completed July 16, 1948.[35] Results of other wells drilled shortly after the Schattel field discovery proved disappointing since four dry holes were put down in the vicinity.[36] During the summer and early fall of 1948 drilling continued near Snyder, and in November, Magnolia Petroleum's number 1 Winston was completed as the discovery well in the Kelley field, also producing from the Canyon lime.[37]

The Winston well initiated a further search for oil in Scurry County. By 1952, 38 distinct reservoirs producing from 13 different stratigraphic positions had been uncovered. The Texas Railroad Commission officially recognized 23 separate fields in the 86,200-acre producing area.[38] Although two wells were proven producers by the end of 1948, it was still not thought that the field would reach large proportions.

Late in November the North Snyder field was opened by Standard of Texas, and it was generally assumed that the field would be limited to the rather large holdings of this company surrounding the discovery test.[39] The principal reason for the pessimistic attitude of oilmen toward these new discoveries was that previous Pennsylvanian fields in the Permian Basin had proved to be small in area and rather disappointing in crude yield.

The Canyon Reef formations of Pennsylvanian age in Scurry County were unlike those previously found because the field was not

[35] The well flowed 149 barrels of 44.2-degree gravity oil in seven hours through a one-half–inch choke on bottom and one-fourth–inch top opening. At this rate its potential was more than 500 barrels a day (*Oil and Gas Journal*, XLVII [July 15, 1948], 60).

[36] *World Oil*, CXXX (April, 1950), 41.

[37] *Oil and Gas Journal*, XLVII (July 22, 1948), 60, and (September 16, 1948), 49. The lease on which the well was drilled was due to expire before the end of the month. The well actually passed up promising pay at 6,800 feet in the Canyon lime and was completed in the 7,400-foot Strawn (*World Oil*, CXXX [February, 1950], 62).

[38] Herald, *Occurrence of Oil and Gas*, p. 295.

[39] *World Oil*, CXXX (February, 1950), 62. The discovery well in the North Snyder field indicated the presence of a gross oil column 764 feet thick (*World Oil*, CXXXI [September, 1950], 73)!

only a large one, but it also was a prolific producer. The productive structure was an elongated buildup of reef that probably began its growth in Strawn time with the greatest development taking place during Canyon time.[40] The entire field, as eventually determined, was mainly in Scurry County, beginning near the southwest corner and extending just west of the town of Snyder, an area about 32 miles long and 4 to 8 miles wide.[41] The oil discoveries in Scurry County made it one of the most important oil-producing counties in the Permian Basin.

Throughout the fifties drilling continued at an unprecedented rate in the Scurry County field with a number of new pools being discovered. By the end of 1953 there were 2,322 wells in the field, yearly production was 44,961,345 barrels, and in the five years after the discovery well had been completed, cumulative production was 187,107,924 barrels of oil.[42] Reserves in the tremendous field were estimated at almost 2,000,000,000 barrels.[43] The boom that resulted from these discoveries as nearly approached the oil mania of the Spindletop and Ranger boom days as anything in recent years. The rush of people to Scurry County taxed the facilities of Snyder since the oil production made inadequate the transportation facilities of the area.[44]

Whereas oil had been found as early as 1926 in Ector County, by 1944 neighboring Midland County was still awaiting its first producing well. In the intervening years Midland had become an oil center, capitalizing on the business that petroleum had brought into the Permian Basin, but no oil was actually being produced in the county. The first such production was found in the Humble Oil and Refining Company's number 1 Mrs. O. P. Buchanan in November 1945.[45]

[40] Herald, *Occurrence of Oil and Gas*, p. 295.

[41] *World Oil*, CXXX (April, 1950), 41.

[42] Herald, *Occurrence of Oil and Gas*, p. 302.

[43] Fancher, *Oil Resources*, p. 304.

[44] By 1950 the Snyder area was served by two eight-inch and two six-inch pipelines, and four new lines were to be built in addition to a ten-inch carrier from the area (*World Oil*, CXXX [April, 1950], 45).

[45] *Midland* (Texas) *Reporter Telegram*, November 15, 1945; and *Oil and Gas Journal*, XLIV (November 17, 1945), 314.

The well produced 270 barrels of oil during an official twenty-four–hour test from the Strawn lime, but the depth, 10,333 feet, and difficulty with salt water caused abandonment of the site in 1947.[46]

Drilling continued in various parts of Midland County during the next two years, but not until 1949 was a second field discovered. The Clarence Scharbauer field, located on the original ranch of that early settler of the region, was found in February 1949 with the completion of the Texas Company wildcat, the number 1 Clarence Scharbauer *et al.*[47] In October of the same year the Tex-Harvey field, which was eventually to account for most of the Midland County production, was opened.[48] The Tex-Harvey field was productive from the Spraberry sand, an amazing formation that underlay between one and two million acres of West Texas land. The sand was first discovered and identified on the Dawson County ranch of Abner J. Spraberry in 1943.[49] There was little interest in the find for a number of years until Seaboard Oil Company drilled a deep test on the ranch in January 1949, which was completed as a 300-barrel a day producer from the Spraberry sand.[50] A second Spraberry well was found in Reagan County, and then one month after the discovery well, Arthur "Tex" Harvey located the sand in Midland County, sixty-five miles south of the Dawson County test.[51]

By 1952 the so-called Spraberry trend had been found in nine

[46] Fancher, *Oil Resources*, p. 296.
[47] *Ibid.*; and *Midland Reporter Telegram*, February 3, 1949.
[48] Fancher, *Oil Resources*, p. 296.
[49] *Midland Reporter Telegram*, March 9, 1952.
[50] Fancher, *Oil Resources*, p. 296. The Spraberry sandstone was a closely compacted and highly fractured one that posed a difficult problem from the first. There was a vast amount of oil in the formation, but initial production declined rapidly, and some method of getting the oil had to be found. Experimentation with new fracturing techniques was somewhat successful (*Oil and Gas Journal*, LII [December 7, 1953], 74).
[51] Fancher, *Oil Resources*, p. 296; and *Midland Reporter Telegram*, March 9, 1952. Estimates of total primary recovery from the Spraberry varied widely, the highest being in the billions of barrels and the most pessimistic indicating that production of the Spraberry trend area would be of limited life and would have to be abandoned within a few years (*Oil and Gas Journal*, LII [June 16, 1952], 64).

counties of West Texas although the majority of the wells located were in Midland, Upton, Glasscock, and Reagan counties. Drilling progressed so rapidly that in the two years following the discovery of the sand 522 wells had been put down. At that time, 1951, the Petroleum Administration for Defense notified operators in the area that enough steel could not be allocated to continue drilling on the forty-acre spacing pattern then in effect.[52] To forestall federal control, operators held a meeting in Fort Worth to propose some plan that would be acceptable to both the federal government and to the Texas Railroad Commission, but the inability of these men to reach an agreement doomed any such proposal.[53]

By the close of 1951 nearly 800 wells had been drilled in the trend area, and new tests were being put down at the rate of 120 a month.[54] Seven pipelines serving the fields handled 1,466,063 barrels of oil during August, and the October allowable set by the Texas Railroad Commission for the fields was about 2,000,000 barrels of oil.[55] The importance of the Spraberry sand was demonstrated by the activities of the Sohio Oil Corporation, which held leases on 44,000 acres in the choice area. During 1951 Sohio spent $10,000,000 in the Spraberry trend and planned to invest an additional $28,000,000 in the area during the following three years.[56]

As suddenly as the boom began, it abruptly, although temporarily, ended in April 1953. The Railroad Commission issued a shutdown order for the entire Spraberry area, effective April 1, which would prevent what it termed wasteful flaring of gas. Operators in the field

[52] *Oil and Gas Journal*, L (October 5, 1951), 150–151.

[53] In July 1951 Magnolia Petroleum asked the Railroad Commission to approve an eighty-acre spacing pattern as a measure to conserve steel. Opposition on the part of operators and royalty owners prevented the plan's adoption (*ibid.*). By December 1951 more than 75 per cent of owners of producing wells had formed the Spraberry Area Engineering Committee to bring some order into the multitude of information about the trend (*ibid.*, L [December 13, 1951], 65, and I [December 20, 1951], 173).

[54] *Ibid.*, L (December 20, 1951), 173.

[55] *Ibid.*, p. 173.

[56] Spraberry wells averaged 7,500 feet in depth, took about forty-five days to drill, and cost about $90,000 (*Midland Reporter Telegram*, March 9, 1952).

objected to the order and tried to prove that the gas flaring was not wasteful, but the Railroad Commission said that about 200,000,000 cubic feet yearly was being wasted.[57] After resorting to injunctions, restraining orders, suits, and other legal maneuvers, a partial relaxation of the order was approved in May, and some 18,000 to 20,000 barrels a day was produced from the 100,000-barrel a day field.[58] Finally, when objectionable practices had been corrected, the Spraberry fields were allowed to begin full production once again.

The Spraberry sand was the largest contributor to Midland County oil production, and by 1952, 5,526,125 barrels had been recovered from the Tex-Harvey field alone.[59] There were also other important discoveries made in the county. In October 1949 the Pegasus field of Upton County was extended into Midland County, and by 1954 had 229 producing wells.[60] The deep production in this field from the Bend and Ellenberger series would not have been possible a few years before because of the drilling expense. The increase in the demand for oil and in prices for crude following the war made it profitable for major companies to invest the approximately $300,000 needed to complete such 11,000- to 14,000-feet wildcats.[61]

Two other minor oil fields were discovered in Midland County during 1950. The Sweetie Peck–Warsan pool was opened March 4, 1950, by the General American Company, and three years later a second pay zone was found in the Pennsylvanian in the southwest corner of the pool.[62] In June 1950 the relatively small Parks field was located and by 1952 had 41 producing wells.[63]

---

[57] *Drill Bit*, I (May, 1953), 48.

[58] Those allowed to resume production had demonstrated that they were not wasting the gas (*ibid.*).

[59] *Midland Reporter Telegram*, March 9, 1952.

[60] At the end of 1954 yearly production in the field was 2,747,578 barrels and cumulative production was 21,353,169 barrels (Herald, *Occurrence of Oil and Gas*, p. 276).

[61] *World Oil*, CXXVIII (October, 1948), 45.

[62] Fancher, *Oil Resources*, p. 296; and Herald, *Occurrence of Oil and Gas*, p. 338.

[63] Herald, *Occurrence of Oil and Gas*, pp. 259–260.

Midland County had only three producing wells at the beginning of 1950, but by 1951 was producing 14,260,578 barrels of oil.[64] The amount of future production and the extent of the reserves of the county could not be accurately estimated because the success of secondary recovery methods in the Spraberry sandstone was unknown. No matter what the results in the Spraberry area might be, Midland County, without a single well in 1945, had become a major oil-producing county in West Texas by 1954.

Dawson County, although the site of the first Spraberry discovery, had less production than most of the counties under consideration. Oil was first found in 1937 with the discovery of the Scanlon field, sixteen miles northwest of Lamesa.[65] This well produced only a short time and was plugged. The field was then inactive until 1941 when Ray A. Albaugh reopened activity by drilling the number 1 J. J. Handley.[66] Eventually 160 wells were completed in the Scanlon pool.[67] In 1949 Seaboard Oil's number 2 S. E. Lee located the Spraberry sand, and an intensive drilling campaign began.[68] A number of smaller fields were discovered in 1951 in Dawson County, but none were large producers. By 1952 total production from Dawson County wells totaled 20,210,079 barrels, and total reserves were 29,383,503.[69]

In addition to the six counties with which this study is particularly interested, other counties in the general area were also important producers of oil. Andrews County had one of the largest productive areas, 103,900 acres of the county's land having been proven capable of yielding oil.[70] Oil was first discovered in the county in 1929, and by 1954 cumulative production reached 301,233,555 barrels with

[64] *Midland Reporter Telegram,* March 9, 1952.

[65] *San Angelo Standard Times,* July 28, 1937.

[66] When reopened the field was called Welch (*Oil and Gas Journal,* XL [December 2, 1941], 74).

[67] Fancher, *Oil Resources,* p. 281.

[68] *Midland Reporter Telegram,* March 9, 1952.

[69] Fancher, *Oil Resources,* p. 281. As in the case of Midland County, the reserves of the Spraberry sand cannot be estimated accurately.

[70] Fancher, *Oil Resources,* p. 274.

nearly 1,500,000,000 barrels of reserves.[71] Gaines County immediately north of Andrews, was the only other area with oil reserves of major proportions. At the end of 1952 Gaines County oil wells had produced 93,469,569 barrels, and reserves were estimated at 530,534,010 barrels.[72]

In 1930 the Permian Basin dominated the drilling picture in the United States. At that time it was the most active drilling area in the world, outranking every state except Texas itself, from the standpoint of well completions and rigs running. During the first half of 1950 completions in the Basin were 46 per cent more than in 1949, while the United States as a whole was reporting a rise of less than 9 per cent. This tremendous activity resulted in the completion of 2,665 new wells in the first half of the year, and at the end of June 1950, there were 722 rigs running in the Permian Basin.[73]

The amazing discoveries made in West Texas during the twenty-year period after the first well was drilled in Mitchell County added an estimated 26,000,000,000 barrels of oil to the nation's reserves.[74] However, all of this petroleum could not be recovered by primary means, nor even by the secondary methods of recovery then known. About 5,000,000,000 barrels could be recovered by primary meth-

[71] *Ibid.* The biggest year of production was 1953 when more than $100,000,000 worth of oil was produced (*Drill Bit*, II [May, 1954], 15).

[72] Fancher, *Oil Resources*, p. 285. Borden County had total production of 9,728,745 barrels and reserves of 29,529,606 barrels (*ibid.*, p. 276). Mitchell County's production was 15,767,520 barrels and reserves were 33,844,741 barrels (*ibid.*, p. 297). The Colorado City "Sunflower Field" on the outskirts of the Mitchell County seat was an oil industry freak. Known for many years, the discovery date of the field was set as 1951 by the Railroad Commission, and the field allowable was set at 21 barrels a day. Oil was found in an area of about 200 acres at a depth of 18 inches. The usual method of recovery was to dig a hole with a posthole digger, let the oil seep in, and pump it out into a settling tank. The oil probably comes through a fault from some deeper formation. Norman Durham, W. K. Crews, and R. L. Moore all produced oil from the field (*Drill Bit*, I [May, 1953], 21).

[73] *World Oil*, CXXXI (September, 1950), 72–73.

[74] These estimates were made by the American Petroleum Institute (*Drill Bit*, I [April, 1953], 21).

ods, and an additional 10,000,000,000 barrels by secondary means.[75]

Although a number of secondary recovery methods were tried in West Texas, gas injection and water flooding were the most satisfactory. The first known gas injection in the Permian Basin was in Ward County in 1930, but the project was abandoned in 1941 when the gas supply failed.[76] Between that time and 1950 a number of similar attempts to increase production of pools lacking a natural gas cap or water drive were undertaken.[77] In 1947 the injection of salt water into the Chalk sand reservoir of the Howard-Glasscock field was begun on a pilot basis since the reservoir had no gas cap at all at the time of discovery. The results caused expansion of the project, and in addition, water was injected into the Yates formation beginning in late 1950.[78]

When discovered, the North Cowden field in Ector County had a natural gas cap, but because of the low permeability of the producing zone, it was decided in 1948 to initiate a gas-injection program. This twenty-year project was the first of its kind on a cooperative and pool-wide basis. The objectives of the plan were to increase ultimate recovery of oil from the Grayburg lime and to make the best use of reservoir gas energy. It was estimated that oil recovery would be increased by 50 per cent. About four-fifths of the acreage in the field was concerned in the project whose principal operators were major oil companies. About 65 input wells, fairly uniformly distributed throughout the field, were used to inject the gas. An outstanding contribution to the operation was made by Cities Service Oil Company, which agreed to share ownership of its twelve-year-old

[75] *Ibid.*, p. 21.
[76] *Ibid.*
[77] Sunray, Magnolia, and Monaday Oil companies all began projects in Winkler County between 1940 and 1945 which were later dropped. Stanolind began a program in Ector County in 1942, and by 1952 there were eighteen such undertakings in West Texas (*Drill Bit*, I [April, 1953], 21–22). In 1953 plans were made to inject gas into the Ellenberger of the Pegasus field in Midland County. The 13,000-foot depth would set a record for such operations (Herald, *Occurrence of Oil and Gas*, p. 271).
[78] Fancher, *Oil Resources*, p. 290.

natural gasoline plant with other operators.[79] About 50 per cent of the gas in the field was returned to the reservoir, and total gas injected up to 1953 was 9,577,000 million cubic feet.[80]

In 1953 the Texas Railroad Commission authorized commencement of the largest unitization program in the world in the Scurry County fields. The Scurry Area Canyon Reef Operators Committee (SACROC) estimated that 720,000,000 barrels of oil could be recovered through secondary recovery methods.[81] The need for such a program had been realized after 1950 when the Railroad Commission ordered a bottom hole pressure survey of the field every six months, and it was found that "pressures were dropping abnormally" in the field.[82] The commission then held two hearings in which operators were asked to show why the production rate should not be reduced and asked for explanations of plans for oil and gas conservation.

A water-injection experiment in the Diamond M pool indicated that the reef was adaptable to a secondary recovery program, and SACROC was formed to carry it out. The approximately 47,000 acres in the field were divided into three units with Magnolia, Standard of Texas, and Sun Oil as the operators of the individual segments. Eight other companies were on the advisory board, and 96 per cent of the operators in the county signed the unitization agreement by which each would share in the production of the unit no matter from which wells the oil was produced.[83] The result of these and other secondary recovery projects was to increase substantially the recoverable reserves in the Permian Basin.[84]

The development of these vast oil-producing formations took place in such a short time and was so recent and continuing that its effect is still being felt. Moreover, at the same time that the oil industry was

[79] *Oil and Gas Journal*, XLVII (July 29, 1948), 52.

[80] *Drill Bit*, I (April, 1953), 23.

[81] *Ibid.*, p. 23.

[82] *Ibid.*, p. 20; and *Abilene Reporter News*, August 23, 1953.

[83] *Abilene* (Texas) *Reporter News*, August 23, 1953.

[84] For a summary of statistics regarding oil and gas production as of 1963, see Appendix III.

reaching its peak in West Texas, the area was also sharing in the boom that the United States experienced during World War II and the postwar years. That the feverish drilling activities with their resultant discoveries of oil throughout the Permian Basin affected the life, growth, and economy of the region was evident. The amazing growth of towns already established in the area was the almost direct result of the discovery of oil. The two largest cities under consideration, Midland and Odessa, grew most rapidly and were almost entirely dependent on oil for their continued existence. The discovery of petroleum in West Texas also gave rise to various industries that contributed to the economic growth of the area. That the impact of oil was an important factor for economic growth was obvious. Exactly what the effect was and how great it was must be considered. Perhaps more important, the lasting contribution of the oil industry must be estimated.

CHAPTER EIGHT

INDUSTRY AND BUSINESS IN WEST TEXAS

ALTHOUGH MANUFACTURING and industry accounted for a larger gross product than did agriculture per se in West Texas by 1930, a great deal of that industry was based on agricultural production. Cotton gins, cottonseed-oil mills, and food-processing plants formed a large part of the production picture of the area, and the economy was still basically dependent on farming, ranching, and the resultant wholesale and retail trade of this industry. The discovery of oil in the period after 1920 changed the area from an agricultural to an industrial region and, in so doing, created a set of new and serious problems and aggravated old ones.

The petroleum industry is an inclusive one that refers to a variety of subsidiary and oil-connected businesses. The finding of oil in West Texas spawned a vast industrial empire that included many separate enterprises employing thousands of people. The process of drilling hundreds of wells alone created a need for drilling rigs and crews, oil-well supply companies, drilling mud and oil-well cementing services, the invention and production of new tools for drilling, and a myriad of other goods and services directly connected with the business of drilling and completing wells.

After the wells were successfully completed, a second and equally important industry had to be created. The obvious need for storage and transportation facilities to take the oil from fields to processing plants brought about a demand for tank cars and pipelines which was filled by railroads and pipeline companies operating in the area. The production of oil and gas also resulted in the construction of refineries and natural-gas liquid-products installations in the areas where oil was being found.

Research in recent years opened the new and growing petrochemical industry. In addition to carbon black, which had been produced for many years from natural gas, it was discovered that sulphur, butadiene, styrene, and other chemical substances could be extracted from oil and gas sources. As a result, after oil was found in West Texas, a number of petrochemical plants were opened in the area.

As the full effect of the petroleum industry, including its related occupations, was felt in West Texas, a change took place in the communities of the area. The employment of thousands of people brought an immediate population growth. The almost overnight transformation of small towns into busy cities strained all the facilities in the municipalities involved. The need for housing, office space, wholesale and retail trade outlets, schools, recreational facilities, and all the other accommodations of a modern city were problems that had to be solved as quickly and efficiently as possible.

The first hurdle was presented by the production and sale of the petroleum and natural gas. This aspect of the industry provided probably the greatest direct profits that were realized. Although a great many people were involved in the sale of oil, most of the production was fairly concentrated in the hands of major oil companies. A large number of independents and individuals controlled acreage in areas where oil was found and consequently made a great deal of money. Major operators, however, generally owned most of the leases or gained control of them shortly after discoveries were made.

The cumulative oil production in the area under consideration had reached more than 2,000,000,000 barrels by 1953.[1] Even though major companies realized most of the profits from the sale of oil, people living in the area of the fields prospered either through payrolls paid by companies to drilling crews, through ownership

[1] *Drill Bit*, I (May, 1953), 24.

of royalties, or through the sale of goods and services to the drilling companies.

A real bonanza for the cities in the areas of oil discoveries was the oil-well supply business. Modern drilling and production techniques called for numerous and varied supplies. Perhaps the first groups to appear in an area in which extensive leasing and drilling activities were taking place were the seismic companies. Although there were a number of different companies in this field, all required crews and equipment and spent money in the towns, thus contributing to the income of merchants. In connection with drilling a vast amount of equipment was required—tools, bits, drilling rigs, and pipe. Also needed for drilling and completion procedures were mud and cementing companies. Although most of the work provided was accomplished by nationally organized companies, either a local or an area office had to be set up by each of them from which to operate. Once again, the economy of the cities received the benefits from the presence of these businesses.

One of the first supply companies located in West Texas was the Atlas Supply Company, which established an office in Odessa during the 1927 boom. From that time on more and more sales and service companies connected with the petroleum industry moved to the city until in 1948 total sales of oil-well supplies in Odessa were $98,000,000 excluding pipe, and pipe sales totaled $240,000,000.[2] Odessa and neighboring Midland were unusual in that they were in the center of large productive areas and consequently became headquarters for many supply companies, but the same situation, to a lesser extent, was to be found in nearly every town in the region.

In addition to national organizations, a large number of local companies served the oil industry. Of particular interest were the small manufacturing concerns that directed their products toward the local market. West Texas during the twenties and thirties was a new area to the oil fraternity, and unusual formations and problems were encountered in connection with drilling. To solve these problems, local tool companies put tools on the market designed for

[2] Finas Wade Horton, "A History of Ector County, Texas" (Master's Thesis, University of Texas), p. 91.

Permian Basin drilling.[3] Local companies also manufactured standard products such as storage tanks for oil fields in the area.[4]

Some West Texas concerns prospered greatly during the periods
of boom, and a few even expanded their sales territory to include
more than the local market.[5] The importance of the supply business
was demonstrated by the Permian Basin Oil Show held in Odessa in
1954. More than 400 concerns exhibited their products, all designed
for use by the petroleum industry, and 150,000 people visited the
exhibition.[6]

Even the cities not located near oil fields sometimes benefited from
the oil boom. No oil was actually discovered in Midland County
until 1945, but during the late twenties and the thirties Midland
became an oil center. In 1926 Gulf established offices in the city,[7]
and two years later there were enough companies with representatives in the community to convince T. S. Hogan that an office build-

    [3] Gist Specialties Company of Odessa was organized in 1951 and searched
for new methods to solve oil field problems. The company developed the
Plur-Adap, a revolutionary tool that is a casing scratcher. Inventions of the
company were marketed through Cardinal Chemical Company (*Drill Bit*, II
[October, 1954], 41). In 1953 the Industrial Instrument Corporation of Odessa
began manufacture of a bellows-type meter used to determine gas flow in
gasoline plants, transmission systems, and gathering lines (*ibid.*, I [May, 1953],
58). The practice of drilling hardrock formations with reversed circulation of
the mud stream proved successful in the Permian Basin. Weston Sales Company
produced a tool specifically designed to reverse the mud stream without the
need for heavy extra equipment (*ibid.*, II [October, 1954], 42).
    [4] Midwest Equipment Company and the Sivalls Tank Company of Odessa
both handled full lines of storage tanks (*El Paso* [Texas] *Times*, November 11,
1954).
    [5] The Sunshine Iron Works, begun in Odessa in 1926, by 1953 employed 50
people and served a wide market (*Drill Bit*, I [May, 1953], 32). The Industrial
Manufacturing Company of Sweetwater was opened in 1948 with two employees. By 1954 it had an annual payroll of $100,000 (*Sweetwater* [Texas]
Reporter, August 13, 1954). The Western Company of Midland began with
four employees in 1939. Fifteen years later it had ten field service points in
Texas, Oklahoma, and Kansas (*Drill Bit*, II [October, 1954], 94).
    [6] *Odessa* (Texas) *American*, November 6, 1954.
    [7] *Fort Worth Star Telegram*, July 26, 1953.

ing would be successful.[8] In 1935 Humble moved its district offices from McCamey to Midland, and a number of other companies soon followed.[9] By 1949 the administrative offices of nearly 250 major and independent companies had their headquarters in Midland.[10] The city's Chamber of Commerce was hardly bragging when it took a full-page advertisement in the *Dallas Morning News* under the head, "Your Business Will Prosper, You Will Be Happy In Midland, Headquarters City of the Permian Basin."[11] The principal reason for this development was Midland's central location between counties in which oil was being produced. An oil company having leases and production in a number of West Texas counties found it convenient to have its district headquarters in Midland, from which all its holdings could be administered.

The taxes paid to West Texas counties where major oil discoveries had been made were another source of income from oil companies. All citizens benefited from these payments, for in some cases these new tax sources provided for community facilities that could not have been constructed otherwise. Ector County, as the county having the largest oil production in the area under consideration, also received the greatest amount of taxes from oil companies. By the early fifties the largest single taxpayer in the county was Phillips Petroleum Company, which was assessed about $100,000 a year.[12] In addition, at least five other major oil companies paid taxes of about $75,000 each year.

An important phase of the petroleum industry in West Texas was the development of the transportation and storage facilities for the

[8] *West Texas Today*, IX (March, 1928), 14. An office building was also constructed in Big Spring as a result of the oil boom. In 1929 the six-story Petroleum Building was built at a cost of $190,000. It was financed by local citizens (*Big Spring* [Texas] *Daily Herald*, April 26, 1936).

[9] *Fort Worth Star Telegram*, July 26, 1953.

[10] *Dallas Morning News*, October 23, 1949.

[11] The advertisement listed banking facilities, buildings, industries, transportation facilities, newspapers, and other advantages the city had to offer (*ibid.*, May 22, 1949).

[12] Bureau of Business Research, University of Texas, Ector County File.

oil and gas produced. Mitchell County, site of the first commercial
well in the Permian Basin, was also the location of the first pipeline,
one running from the Westbrook field to the railroad siding at Westbrook.[13] Although the original line has long since fallen into disuse,
a series of newer outlets were built in the county, and the Colorado
City Station of the Basin Pipeline Company was an important link
in the oil transportation system of the Basin.[14]

As new fields were opened in West Texas, it was necessary to
build lines immediately, and a number of new pipelines opened.
Typical of the quick action of pipeline companies was that of Shell
Pipeline in 1948 after the discovery of Midland County's TXL field.
Within a month of the completion of the discovery well, Shell had
constructed lateral lines to the field from its ten-inch West Texas-
Oklahoma carrier.[15] Activity also quickened in Scurry County following the completion of the Winston well in 1948, and within two years
there were twelve lines in the county, and construction or plans for
an additional nine outlets had been begun.[16] These new facilities
were generally owned by a major company or by a combination of
companies that owned a long carrier on an undivided interest basis.

Such cooperative ownership and use of carriers from the West
Texas area was not unusual. In May 1953 the Rancho Pipe Line
System was officially opened. The 457-mile line, with an initial ca-
pacity of 210,000 barrels a day, was jointly owned by seven com-
panies.[17] In the same month, what was then the largest pipeline in
North America, the 578-mile, 26-inch line of the West Texas Gulf
Pipe Line Company was dedicated. The carrier was owned by five

[13] *Drill Bit*, II (May, 1954), 13.
[14] The Basin Pipeline System, operated by the Texas Pipe Line Company
was owned by the Texas, Sinclair, Cities Service, and Shell Pipe Line Companies. The maximum pumping capacity of the station, which gathered oil
from fields in Scurry, Kent, Borden, and Howard counties, was 350,000 barrels
a day. The station was almost completely automatic and was operated by
twelve men (*ibid.*).
[15] *World Oil*, CXXVIII (October, 1948), 45.
[16] *Ibid.*, CXXX (April, 1950), 45.
[17] *Drill Bit*, I (May, 1953), 39.

separate companies.[18] By 1954 there were sixteen major carriers moving oil from the Permian Basin.[19] These lines varied from 8 to 26 inches in diameter and had a combined capacity of 1,674,600 barrels daily.[20] Besides these major outlets, a network of smaller lateral lines was constructed in every field in the area.

Another product of the oil fields of West Texas, natural gas, was also transported through pipelines, with the El Paso Natural Gas Company as the largest purchaser in the area. El Paso Natural not only owned part interest in pipelines but also constructed its own carriers. In 1948 the organization signed a commitment with operators in Midland County fields to purchase a minimum of 20,000,000 cubic feet of gas daily for a period of twenty-five years.[21] To transport the gas, about 100 miles of pipelines were extended from the fields to the company's Jal, New Mexico, station.[22]

These carriers almost constituted a separate industry in themselves. Besides the profits of the companies owning and operating the pipelines, the purchase of materials and the employment of construction crews to build the outlets created an additional income for the area. After the completion of pipelines, permanent crews for maintenance and operations were hired, although the total number was not large since a great deal of automation was involved in operation of the equipment.

It was only natural that with the discovery of oil in the Permian Basin a number of petroleum-connected industries would spring up. Although the first oil was found in 1920, it was not until the late

[18] *Ibid.*, p. 56. The line was owned by Gulf Refining, Cities Service, Sun, Standard of Ohio, and Pure Oil companies (*ibid.*).

[19] *Drill Bit*, II (May, 1954), 59.

[20] In April 1954 the line moved 1,210,570 barrels of oil. A little more than half was shipped to the east-southeast, and the remainder to the north-northwest (*ibid.*).

[21] *World Oil*, CXXVIII (October, 1948), 50.

[22] The contract became effective October 1, 1949, but if the line had not been completed at that time, producers were to be paid $250.00 a day as penalties. El Paso Natural also advanced producers $3,000,000 for construction of a gasoline plant (*ibid.*).

twenties that any major oil discoveries were made. By that time a
few refineries had been built to process West Texas crude, but most
of them had a short history and went out of business within a few
years.[23] By 1954 there were seven refineries in the Permian Basin
area, and three of them, those at Sweetwater, Big Spring, and Colorado City, were in the counties under consideration.[24] Of these
processing plants, only one, the Cosden Refinery at Big Spring, was
equipped to serve more than a local market.

The Cosden Refinery was one of the earliest constructed after the
discovery of oil in West Texas. Originally built in 1929, the plant
was profitable during its first years of existence, but by the mid-
thirties low prices for refinery products were cutting into profits.
As a result, Cosden scientists began searching for other uses for crude
oil and in 1935 placed an asphalt unit in operation at the Big Spring
plant.[25] Results during the first six months of operation were so good
that the capacity of the new installation was doubled.

By 1947 the Cosden Refinery was a mainstay of the Big Spring
economy. At that time the plant employed 375 people and produced
petroleum products with an estimated total value of $12,000,000.[26]
The operation continued to grow, and in 1951 a new low-stage crude
distillation unit, which increased the crude charging capacity of the
refinery by 20 per cent, was placed in production.[27] In the following year a new $3,250,000 unit for the manufacture of benzene,
toluene, and xylene was opened, and in 1953 ground was broken to
begin construction of a $2,750,000 addition for the production of
high-grade aviation gasoline.[28]

Cosden maintained its position as an important refinery in West
Texas, serving a growing market area through the midwest and

[23] *Oil and Gas Journal,* XXIX (September, 1930), 73.
[24] *Ibid.,* LII (August 6, 1954), 45.
[25] The capacity when doubled was 2,000 barrels a day (*ibid.,* XXXIV [June 20, 1935], 18).
[26] The Cosden plant accounted for about 95 per cent of the employees and of the gross product of manufacturing in Big Spring (Bureau of Business Research, University of Texas, Howard County File).
[27] *Oil and Gas Journal,* L (October 4, 1951), 324.
[28] *Fort Worth Star Telegram,* October 4, 1953.

southwest, by continual research and expansion. In 1953 more than 600 people were employed at the Big Spring plant, and the annual payroll was more than $3,000,000.[29] Three years later the processing plant handled over 27,000 barrels of Permian Basin crude each day.[30] At the time $11,000,000 in capital improvements were either under construction or contract, and the company had recently purchased the six-floor Petroleum Building for its headquarters.[31]

The success of Cosden in refining and marketing petroleum products was not the usual story of such plants in West Texas. Perhaps more typical was the Howard County Refining Company, which was opened in 1928.[32] This plant handled 880,000 barrels of oil during the first year of operation, but when emphasis of oilmen switched to East Texas in 1931, the plant began gradually to lose money and finally went out of business.

Also typical of the refineries that were unable to keep up with changing times was the Gulf Refinery at Sweetwater. Built in 1929, the Gulf installation eventually became the victim of advanced technology and was forced to cease operations in 1954. At that time the plant employed 96 people and for a number of years had produced regular-grade gasoline as its highest octane product.[33] Not affected by the closing of the Gulf Refinery was an agreement between the company and the city of Sweetwater by which the oil concern had agreed to help finance the new Oak Creek Lake by purchasing water for a period of thirty years.[34] This contract demonstrated two aspects of the oil industry in West Texas: the willingness in many cases of oil corporations to cooperate with municipalities in civic improvements, and the need for water for the operation of nearly any petroleum-connected industry.[35]

[29] *Ibid.*

[30] *West Texas Today*, XXXVII (May, 1956), 12; and *San Angelo* (Texas) *Standard Times*, August 4, 1956.

[31] *West Texas Today*, XXXVII (May, 1956), 12.

[32] *Big Spring Daily Herald*, April 26, 1936.

[33] *Drill Bit*, II (May, 1954), 55; and *Amarillo* (Texas) *Daily News*, September 23, 1954.

[34] *Amarillo Daily News*, September 23, 1954.

[35] *Dallas Morning News*, October 23, 1949.

Almost from the time of the first oil discoveries in the Permian Basin there were industries in operation dependent on oil and gas wells for their existence. Both the 1928 and 1931 editions of *Mineral Resources of the United States* reported the production of natural gasoline in West Texas.[36] From that time on an increasing number and variety of industries were begun in the West Texas area, until in the forties and fifties nearly every county was the site of a plant of some type.

By far the largest number of plants constructed were the natural gasoline operations. These installations made use of the gas from oil and gas wells by stripping the "wet" gasses of their liquid hydrocarbons and thus preparing them for transmission through pipelines.[37] As new fields were discovered, gasoline plants were often built, and the production of butane, propane, and natural gasoline became an important industry in the region.[38] Natural gasoline production units were also installed in connection with repressuring projects in various fields, thus making a dual use of the gas forced back into oil-bearing formations.

One of the processes longest associated with the petroleum industry has been that of producing carbon black.[39] During World War II, when there was a great demand for synthetic rubber, the United States Government built a large carbon black plant near Odessa.[40] The installation, built at a cost of $9,000,000 and leased to Union Carbide Company, was purchased by the operator follow-

[36] *Mineral Resources of the United States,* 1928, Part II: Non-Metals, p. 212; and 1931, Part II: Non-Metals, p. 337.

[37] *World Oil,* CXXX (May, 1950), 47.

[38] Typical of the plants processing natural gas were those in Nolan County: the Rowan and Hope $500,000 plant built in 1953 and purchased by Sinclair in 1956; an installation near the White Flat field built in 1955; and three plants built in 1956 near Maryneal (*Sweetwater Reporter,* August 13, and December 22, 1953, January 8 and May 16, 1956). Scurry County had four gasoline plants by 1954 (*Fort Worth Star Telegram,* February 21, 1954; *Drill Bit,* II [October, 1954], 26). More than thirty gasoline plants were in operation in West Texas in 1954 (Horton, "History of Ector County," p. 94).

[39] Carbon black is a small particle pigment produced by burning gas in a deficiency of air (*Drill Bit,* I [October, 1954], 66).

[40] *West Texas Today,* XIX (August, 1947), 6.

ing the war, and by 1950 production capacity was increased to 56,000,000 pounds of channel black yearly.[41] In 1953 a second Ector County carbon black plant was opened, the Sid Richardson Carbon Company unit; it was the largest channel plant in the world at that time.[42] By this date there were ten such factories in the Permian Basin, half of them in the area under consideration.[43]

Research in petrochemicals led to the founding of another industry in West Texas, the extraction of sulphur. A great deal of the gas produced in the Permian Basin was "sour" gas of limited use because of its offensive odor and corrosive qualities. In 1952 Phillips Petroleum Company began construction of a plant at Goldsmith, Ector County, designed to extract sulphur from such gas.[44] Built at a cost of $1,741,000, the plant produced 125 tons of elemental sulphur daily; this in turn was used to make ammonium sulphate in the Phillips plant at Houston.[45]

In 1953 Stanolind Oil and Gas opened a plant in conjunction with its North Cowden gasoline unit for the production of sulphur.[46] This was the eighth sulphur plant in the area, giving the Permian Basin a daily productive capacity of 291 tons.[47] A combination of scientific research and recognition of the commercial possibilities of a

---

[41] Channel black is produced by burning small flames in little air. The smoke impinges on slowly moving iron channels, which in turn pass over fixed scrapers placed in stationary hoppers six feet apart. The carbon black is scraped off into the bottom of each hopper where moving screws convey it to a packing house. There it is mixed with water and agitated to form tiny pellets (Horton, "History of Ector County," p. 94).

[42] *Drill Bit,* I (May, 1953), 39.

[43] The other plants were the Cabot Carbon Company units at Big Spring, Kermit, and Wickett, and the Columbian Carbon Company plant at Seagraves. The Big Spring plant used the oil furnace method of production, in which carbon black is made from oil sprayed into a hot furnace (*ibid.,* p. 41).

[44] The sulphur was taken in a molten state to a plant in Fort Worth and there converted into sulphuric acid to be used in making fertilizer (*Oil and Gas Journal,* L [January 14, 1952], 67).

[45] *Ibid.*

[46] *Drill Bit,* I (April, 1953), 28.

[47] *Fort Worth Star Telegram,* December 16, 1955.

natural product of the area were responsible for the creation of this new industry in West Texas.

The most ambitious and one of the most promising developments in connection with petrochemicals took place in Ector County in 1955. In December of that year, El Paso Natural Gas Company and General Tire and Rubber Company announced completion of a multimillion-dollar agreement to construct the nation's first postwar, privately financed synthetic rubber operation.[48] A complex of three separate plants, the rubber manufacturing factory was completed by 1957. The Odessa Butadiene Company, which manufactures one component used in the production of rubber, began operation in 1957. The $22,000,000 plant produced 50,000 tons of butadiene a year, 75 per cent of which was purchased by General Tire and Rubber Company, the remainder being sold to a rubber plant in Baytown, Texas.[49] A second product needed for the manufacture of rubber was produced by the $6,000,000 installation of the Odessa Styrene Company.[50] Styrene, made from ethylene and benzene, was produced at the rate of 35,000,000 pounds a year from products of the Spraberry field crudes.[51] The third plant in the process was the GR-S copolymer blending operation, which combined the butadiene and styrene in making synthetic rubber.[52]

The construction of the synthetic rubber facilities near Odessa revealed one of the most serious problems connected with industrial expansion in West Texas and brought about a novel solution to that

[48] The plant, employing 150 people, used over 25,000 barrels daily of liquid hydrocarbons (Mark Van Auken of El Paso Natural Gas Products Company, Odessa, letter to Bureau of Business Research, University of Texas, July 14, 1957). El Paso Natural also built a refinery and alkylation unit at Odessa which was connected to El Paso by a 250-mile, six-inch pipeline. About 2,000 barrels daily of by-products from the refinery were converted by the alkylation unit into a blending component for high octane and aviation gasoline (*Wall Street Journal*, March 6, 1957).

[49] *Odessa American*, October 10, 1957.

[50] *Fort Worth Star Telegram*, October 29, 1956; and *West Texas Today*, XXXVII (November, 1956), 26.

[51] *Fort Worth Star Telegram*, October 29, 1956.

[52] This plant cost $12,000,000 (*West Texas Today*, XXXVII [November, 1956], 26).

problem. The butadiene plant required nearly 3,000,000 gallons of water daily for its operation, and the styrene and copolymer units needed lesser amounts.[53] To provide water from the city's supply would have been possible, but dangerous in case the supply should decrease or the city needs should become greater. To solve the difficulty, El Paso Natural Gas Company, Odessa Natural Gasoline Company, and General Tire and Rubber Company signed a contract with the city of Odessa to buy reclaimed water from the sewage system. The agreement called for the three companies to repay the municipality for the construction of a $750,000 secondary sewage treatment plant and after the plant was paid for to continue purchasing water at the rate of 4,000,000 gallons a day for a period of twenty years.[54] This settlement of a common problem worked well for both the city and the industry.

Big Spring's Cosden Refinery was the site of the Permian Basin's second styrene plant. In 1955 it was announced that the refinery would construct facilities in a gamble that styrene could be produced directly from ethylbenzene recovered from gasoline.[55] The $3,000,000 installation was completed successfully in January 1957 and was run on complete automation with only two men at the controls.[56]

Although manufacturing and processing in connection with petroleum became the most important industry in the Permian Basin, it was neither the first nor the only source of manufactured goods. Other mineral resources of the area and agricultural production gave rise to industry in West Texas. As early as 1939 there were 76 manufacturing establishments in the six counties under consideration producing goods valued at more than $8,000,000.[57] These figures

[53] *San Angelo Standard-Times,* January 26, 1956.

[54] *Ibid.*

[55] *Abilene Reporter News,* September 19, 1955. The plant was equipped to produce 20,000,000 pounds of styrene a year. The process used was a new one, and there was some question as to the success at first (*Fort Worth Star Telegram,* March 14, 1956).

[56] *San Angelo Standard-Times,* April 3, 1957.

[57] There were 921 employees in these factories. The total wages annually were $708,601. The figure for wages and value of products does not include that

included a number of small plants of various types and at least one important industry, the United States Gypsum Company at Sweetwater.

The presence of excellent deposits of gypsum rock and gypsite in Nolan County had caused the United States Gypsum Company to build the plant at Sweetwater in 1923.[58] The factory, which produced paints, wallboard, plasters, and cements, was expanded a number of times, the most important addition being made in 1950 when a $1,500,000 expansion was completed.[59] By 1954 the gypsum company employed 500 people and had an annual payroll of $2,000,000.[60]

The United States Gypsum Company plant was the only such installation in Nolan County for more than twenty-five years, but in the fifties the mineral deposits of the area attracted other companies. In 1950 the Lone Star Cement Company announced plans for construction of a plant at Maryneal near Sweetwater.[61] Completed in 1951, the $7,000,000 facilities had a productive capacity yearly of 2,500,000 barrels of cement.[62] After three years of operation, the Lone Star factory employed nearly 200 men, most of whom made their homes in Sweetwater.[63]

In 1954 a small factory was built in Sweetwater by the Texcrete Company. The $250,000 plant produced masonry products to be sold in a 200-mile radius of Sweetwater.[64] When production began in

---

for Howard County which was not given because it would reveal details of the financial structure of companies in the county. Food-processing and printing plants accounted for the greatest number of establishments although these did not necessarily produce goods of the greatest value (*Sixteenth Census of the United States, 1940: Manufacturing*, III, 983–984).

[58] *Sweetwater Reporter*, August 13, 1954.

[59] *Ibid.*, April 2, 1950.

[60] *Ibid.*, August 13, 1954.

[61] The company took full-page advertisements headed "A New Star Is Born" to announce the proposed plant (*Dallas Times Herald*, October 8, 1950; and *Dallas Morning News*, March 30, 1950).

[62] *Abilene Reporter News*, March 14, 1951.

[63] Plant capacity was increased 50 per cent in 1953 (*Fort Worth Star Telegram*, September 27, 1953).

[64] *Sweetwater Reporter*, December 14, 1954.

September 1954, the plant was almost completely automatic and consequently required few employees.

Three years after the Texcrete factory opened, a second gypsum plant was constructed near Sweetwater by the Flintkote Gypsum Company. When the Flintkote installation was completed, it employed about 200 people and had an annual payroll of $1,000,000.[65] One final industry made use of the mineral deposits in Nolan County. In 1958 the Gifford-Hill Pipe Company announced that it planned to build a factory in Sweetwater for the manufacture of cement pipes.[66] Combined with the petroleum and agricultural industries, these factories helped give a broad base to the economy of the area and to provide employment for a large number of people.

Railroads also accounted for large payrolls in Howard and Nolan counties. For many years the Texas and Pacific yards and shops, located at Big Spring, were an important factor in the prosperity of the community. In 1956 nearly 900 people living in the town were employed by the railroad. Nolan County also benefited from railroads, for shops of the Santa Fe located in Sweetwater employed 200 maintenance personnel from the local labor force at that time.[67]

Agriculture had a double importance in the economy of West Texas. Farmers' incomes were spent mostly with the wholesale and retail establishments in the cities under consideration, and the processing plants for the agricultural production of the area accounted for a second major phase of the industry. Nearly every town, large or small, had at least one cotton gin to handle part of the local production. In Lamesa, county seat of Dawson County, which was the largest cotton producer in the area, there were 22 cotton gins and 2 compresses in 1949.[68]

Sweetwater had one of the largest industries dependent on agriculture, the Sweetwater Cotton Oil Company. The plant, located on a seventy-five–acre tract north of the town, included a feed mill,

[65] The plant cost $5,000,000 (*San Angelo Standard-Times*, September 19, 1957).

[66] *Sweetwater Reporter*, May 5, 1958.

[67] *Ibid.*, April 6, 1956.

[68] *West Texas Today*, XXX (November, 1949), 34.

grain storage facilities, cottonseed-oil mill, insecticide plant, and shops, offices and truck space. At peak production the facilities employed between 150 and 200 people.[69] Other important agriculture-connected industries in the area included three meat-packing plants in Sweetwater where 17,000 cattle and about the same number of hogs were slaughtered and processed annually,[70] grain elevators in nearly every large community, and an egg dehydration plant in Lamesa.[71]

By 1950 manufacturing of agriculture-related products had become so important that it accounted for more employees than any industry except construction and petroleum, both of which were subject to considerable fluctuation.[72] Although not primarily an industrial region, West Texas had reached a point where industry made a major contribution to the income sources of the area and added to the diversification of the economy of the region.

The payrolls of federal and state installations in West Texas also contributed to the income of the area. An 890-bed state mental hospital was located two miles north of Big Spring, and in 1950 a 250-bed Veterans Administration hospital was opened in the town.[73] The employment of professional and administrative personnel provided jobs for a large number of people. In addition to these installations, there were two military bases in the area. In 1942 the Webb Air Force Base was constructed at Big Spring at a cost of $17,309,365. At the end of 1958 there were 745 civilian employees at the base, and the annual payroll was nearly $3,250,000. Furthermore, the military payroll of more than $10,000,000 each year was spent to a large extent in Big Spring. The second military installation was at

---

[69] *Sweetwater Reporter*, August 12, 1954. Employment was never steady, for only during the period when cotton was being ginned was there a great demand for workers.

[70] The three companies employed 100 people (*Fort Worth Star Telegram*, September 27, 1953).

[71] *West Texas Today*, XXX (November, 1949), 35.

[72] In the six counties, 8,373 were employed in mining, 4,646 in construction, and 3,833 in industry (*Seventeenth Census of the United States, 1950: Population*, II, 43).

[73] *West Texas Today*, XXXI (July, 1950), 19.

Sweetwater where the Air Force Control and Warning Station M-89 was built in 1955 at a cost of $1,187,000. At the end of fiscal 1958 there were nine civilian employees at the base. The civilian payroll was $38,600 annually, and the military payroll was $641,000.[74]

Although there were other small industries in the cities of West Texas, these were the most important ones and the ones common to most of the area. The beginning of industry on a large scale, particularly that connected with the petroleum-related installations, aggravated the already serious water-supply problem. The use of wells and such surface water sources as existed proved satisfactory for early settlers and for their descendants in the period before 1930. Even in this semiarid region there was little suffering from lack of water except during years of extreme drought. But the oil discoveries of the forties, the large-scale population movement into West Texas, and the industrial growth caused an ever more serious need for locating new sources of water.

A survey of public water supplies in West Texas published by the Texas Board of Water Engineers in 1949, showed that only two of the counties under consideration, Howard and Nolan, had surface lakes as a part of the municipal water supply. Big Spring's Moss Creek Reservoir and Powell Creek Reservoir had a total capacity of 4,100 acre-feet, and Sweetwater's Lake Trammel and Lake Sweetwater had a total surface area of 1,040 acres.[75] The other counties relied entirely on well fields for their water supplies.[76]

The dependence of municipalities in West Texas upon the underground water table formed another aspect of the general problem of obtaining an adequate source of supply. In Ector County the Texas Board of Water Engineers reported that the average daily pumpage from city wells in eleven months of 1949 was over six times greater than for the entire year of 1938.[77] This was not unusual since there had been a tremendous population growth in Odessa

[74] Major General W. P. Fisher, letter to Senator Robert S. Kerr, May 19, 1959.

[75] W. L. Broadhurst, *et al., Public Water Supplies in Western Texas*, pp. 142, 196.

[76] *Ibid.*, pp. 60, 75, 182, 240.

[77] *Ibid.*, pp. 60–61; and D. B. Knowles, *Ground-Water Resources of Ector County, Texas*, p. 14.

between these dates. The important factor was that drillers found the water level had dropped between these terminal dates, indicating a reduction of about 14 per cent in the amount of water in storage. Although Ector County was unusual because its population growth had been great, a similar situation existed in other counties in the area.[78]

Much of the water table of western Texas was formed in ages past by runoff from the Rocky Mountains through water-permeable formations. Later, faults and uplifts broke these sands and made subsequent replenishing of the water table by this means impossible.[79] The only way in which the level could be raised was by percolation from the surface. The semiarid nature of the region made it unlikely that a great amount of water could be had by this means. By the forties when the first industry was beginning to appear in West Texas and when the population was growing rapidly, cities in the area were almost completely dependent on a decreasing underground water supply. Three possible solutions to the water problem existed: (1) the creation of new impounding reservoirs wherever possible, (2) finding new well fields, or (3) cooperative efforts on the part of two or more municipalities to create a common water supply. No matter which solution was chosen, the need for extensive conservation planning was obvious, and the aid of industries in the area was desirable.

Sweetwater chose the first of these methods, the expansion of already existing facilities and the construction of a new reservoir. In 1953 the *Fort Worth Star Telegram* reported that Sweetwater had solved its water problem with the new Oak Creek Reservoir, which had 13,000 acre-feet of water available for city use. The lake, which would have 40,000 acre-feet when filled to capacity, also served the small towns of Bronte and Roby in Nolan County.[80] When available funds were exhausted early in 1953 with seven miles of pipelines still to be built, Gulf Oil advanced $240,000 to make possible the

[78] Broadhurst, *Public Water Supplies*, pp. 75, 182, 196, 240.

[79] Penn Livingston and Robert R. Bennett, *Geology and Ground Water Resources of the Big Spring Area, Texas*, pp. 52–53.

[80] *Fort Worth Star Telegram*, September 27, 1953.

completion of the $2,700,000 project.[81] The Oak Creek Reservoir and all the necessary pumping stations and pipelines were not completed in time for the drought of 1953–1954, and when the available water supplies of Lake Trammel and Lake Sweetwater were exhausted, it was necessary to drill new wells.[82] Although there was some discomfort, the drought did not seriously affect the economy of the town, and in 1954 the lake and its facilities were ready for use.

The other counties in the area faced a problem similar to that of Sweetwater, but most of them had no area suitable for impounding water. Dawson County simply drilled additional wells during the late forties to supplement the supply.[83] Ector County had probably the greatest water problem because of its large population growth. The annual usage of water in Odessa rose from 206,600,000 gallons in 1938 to 1,403,950,000 in 1950.[84] In 1948 a report to Governor Beuford Jester of Texas stated that the only source of supply at that time was from 40 wells, and that the water level was reduced in a very few years. Although the wells produced 6,000,000 gallons daily, it was estimated that by 1980 the city would need 12,500,000 gallons of water each day.[85]

Midland, with a rapidly growing population, faced the same problem as did Odessa, and Big Spring and Snyder had similar but lesser water difficulties. These cities, with the exception of Midland, used a combination of the possible solutions to the water problem by drilling new wells, impounding water, and establishing a municipal water program on a cooperative basis.

As it became more and more obvious in the mid-forties that some solution had to be found if the towns were to continue in existence, Odessa hired a firm of water engineers, Freese and Nichols, to make an intensive study of available water in West Texas. The firm located a new field in Martin County and recommended a dam site on the Colorado River in Scurry County. Since the expense involved in

[81] Gulf had agreed to buy water from the city (*ibid.*).

[82] Increased water rates and rationing were used as conservation measures (*Abilene Reporter News*, May 25, 1954).

[83] Broadhurst, *Public Water Supplies*, p. 60.

[84] Knowles, *Ground-Water Resources of Ector County*, p. 16.

[85] Texas, State Board of Water Engineers, Austin, Texas, Ector County File.

constructing a lake one hundred miles away would be prohibitive, it was decided to bring other cities into the project.[86] In October 1946 a permit was issued by the State Board of Water Engineers for Colorado City, Big Spring, Snyder, Odessa, and Midland to form a water-control improvement district and to appropriate 30,000 acre-feet of water each year by building a dam across the Colorado River and thereby impounding 111,000 acre-feet of water.[87]

In February 1949 official ceremonies were held to begin construction of the dam, and in May the state legislature passed a bill setting up the Colorado River Municipal Water District (CRMWD), consisting originally of Odessa and Big Spring.[88] Elections held in these cities in July brought the overwhelming approval of the program by the electorate, and the following year Snyder was added to the district after an election in that municipality.[89]

Big Spring began using water from the CRMWD well field in 1952, and from that time on there was no need for water rationing in the city.[90] A year later Odessa was obtaining, at peak consumption, 10,800,000 gallons of water daily from Ector and Martin County wells owned by the district. The city, which had rationed water in the summers of 1951 and 1952, could use 15,000,000 gallons a day from the Martin County wells alone. To assure adequate storage facilities, the city was constructing a storage tank to hold 85,000,000 gallons, and later total storage facilities were to be expanded to 300,000,000 gallons.[91]

---

[86] *Odessa American,* August 6, 1951.

[87] This permit was the result of a petition from representatives of these cities who held a meeting in June to discuss the proposed plan. J. B. Thomas of Fort Worth, president of the Texas Electric Service Company, presided at the meeting and spearheaded the entire program (Texas, State Board of Water Engineers, Austin, Texas, Colorado River Municipal Water District File).

[88] *Ibid.*

[89] The beginning of the project was approved by the following votes in each city: Odessa, 365 for and 16 against; Big Spring, 522 for and 31 against; and Snyder, 402 for and 25 against. There was apparently little real interest among the electorate in the election (*ibid.*).

[90] *Fort Worth Star Telegram,* October 4, 1953.

[91] *Ibid.,* July 5, 1953.

The first water from Lake J. B. Thomas on the Colorado River was purchased by nearby Snyder in 1953.[92] At the time the city was getting about one-third of its supply from the lake, and after a new $300,000 filter plant was completed, the entire city water supply would come from the lake.[93] By 1955 the CRMWD served the three original towns, two representing groups of rural users, the community of Coahoma near Big Spring, the SACROC and Sharon Ridge repressuring projects in Scurry County, the Texas-Gulf Refinery in Ector County, and a number of individual rural residents and drilling companies.[94] More than 7,000,000,000 gallons of water, about three-fifths of it from Lake Thomas, was sold during the year.

Financially the CRMWD proved to be a success. The original bond issue of $11,750,000, which provided for the construction of the lake, development of well fields, and building necessary pipelines and pumping stations, was easily sold. Between 1952 and 1954 revenues were $1,226,495.60 and expenses $904,982.80. In 1955 total revenue was more than $1,000,000, and in 1957 total assets of the district were $24,555,670 and total liabilities just over $11,000,000.[95]

Midland, after temporarily considering joining the Colorado River project, decided to pursue an independent course of action in the search for water. In 1948 all of the county's water came from fourteen wells that produced about 5,000,000 gallons a day. At that time it was estimated that the requirements of Midland would be 10,000,000 gallons daily by 1960.[96] Since the underground table was the only source of supply, the city began an intensive search for water in 1950 and three years later had invested about $2,000,000

[92] The original permit was amended to allow a lake of 204,000 acre-feet (*Abilene Reporter News*, August 23, 1953).

[93] *Ibid.*, August 23, 1953.

[94] *Ibid.*, January 14, 1956.

[95] About half of the revenue came from Odessa (Texas, State Board of Water Engineers, Austin, Texas, Colorado River Municipal Water District File).

[96] These estimates were later proved to be less than the actual requirements of the city (*ibid.*, Midland County File).

in the project.[97] A number of suitable locations for new well fields were found within the county and water rights were purchased. The city appeared to have followed a shortsighted course in refusing to join the CRMWD in 1951, for the reasons given were that the city's water supply would be taken over by the district and that a large indebtedness would be incurred.[98] Since the city invested $2,000,000 in the search for water by 1953, and even then was not certain that a permanent supply had been found, the previous action seemed a mistake.

In 1955 Midland was once again considering a municipal water project, this time the proposed Canadian River program, which would involve a dam site 275 miles north of Midland.[99] This plan never progressed beyond the talking stage, and in 1956 Midland officials announced that partial results of a water exploration program indicated that underground supplies capable of sustaining a population of 150,000 had been found in Martin County.[100] The city obtained an option to purchase water rights on 20,000 acres in that area, thirty miles northwest of Midland. The Midland city officials felt that the water problem had been solved, but continual dependence on wells to supply a growing urban area was at best a risky undertaking.

The need for water in West Texas was greater in 1958 than it had been when the first settlers pushed their way out onto the Texas plains, and it was becoming greater with each passing year. In the eighteen-seventies there were few people, and they could exist on water found in springs and creeks. By the middle of the twentieth century the oil-laden lands of West Texas supported a large and increasing population and a growing industrialization that were entirely dependent on an adequate water supply for their existence.

[97] *Ibid.*
[98] *Midland Reporter Telegram*, March 9, 1952.
[99] Texas, State Board of Water Engineers, Austin, Texas, Canadian River Water District File.
[100] *San Angelo Standard-Times*, October 24, 1955.

CHAPTER NINE

THE CITIES: Past, Present, and Future

BOTH THE GROWTH in the number of people and the industrialization of West Texas were largely the result of the discovery of oil. In a few of the counties under consideration agriculture remained an important, indeed a basic, industry, but in those areas showing a large population, increased oil production was the major factor in the economy. The rise in the population of individual cities was almost directly proportional to the amount of oil activity in the county. Industry was also a factor in the development of the economy of West Texas, but with the exception of the gypsum industries in Nolan County, nearly all manufacturing in the region was connected in some way with petroleum. In 1930 oil production in the Permian Basin had barely begun. By 1958 cities that were to be affected by oil activity had felt the full impact of the petroleum industry and had changed accordingly.

Between 1930 and 1940 the population of Big Spring decreased from 13,735 to 12,604.[1] During this decade there was little oil activity other than the extension of already discovered fields, and the economy suffered the general effects of the depression. Agriculture, still of primary importance during the thirties, was hurt by the drought during these years, and in 1940 production of crops was less than it had been ten years before.[2] By this date there were only

[1] U.S., Department of Commerce, Bureau of the Census, *Sixteenth Census of the United States, 1940: Population*, I, 1057.

[2] *Ibid., Agriculture*, I, Part V, 465, 485.

802 farms in the county, 24 of which had some irrigated land, and the value of all crops was $1,216,684.[3] Ranching maintained its former position, and 17,543 cattle and 23,659 sheep were grazed on ranches in Howard County.[4] Economic development in the area had almost come to a standstill, and had it not been for the little oil activity that did take place, the population loss for the decade might have been greater.

Construction almost stopped during the depression years in Big Spring, and building permits averaged about $100,000 a year for the decade.[5] In 1938 the citizens did support a bond issue of $275,000 which was combined with $225,000 supplied by the Public Works Administration for the construction of the Moss Creek Dam.[6] Little work was to be had, and 287 people in the county were engaged in public emergency work for the United States in 1940.[7] The principal business in the town was retail trade, which accounted for sales of $9,833,000 in 1939.[8]

The economic picture in Howard County did not brighten until the mid-forties. Indicative of the return of a measure of prosperity were the increased number of building permits, which were valued at $778,223 in 1945 and passed the $1,000,000 mark the following year. Farm production also began to rise during the forties. In 1947 the Howard County agent reported that there were 753 farms in the county, of which 313 were operated by tenants. Cotton, to which 65 per cent of cropland was devoted, accounted for most of the farm income of $3,750,000 in 1946. The value of cattle on ranches at the time was $1,749,000.[9] Retail sales, a final barometer of the return of business activity, reached $28,753,000 in 1948.[10]

Accompanying the business developments was an increase in population. By 1950 there were 17,286 people in Big Spring, and more

[3] *Ibid.*, p. 342.
[4] *Ibid.*, p. 433.
[5] *Big Spring* (Texas) *Daily Herald*, January 2, 1941.
[6] *Ibid.*, December 7, 1938.
[7] *Sixteenth Census of the United States, 1940: Population*, I, 878.
[8] *Ibid.*, *Business*, I, 458.
[9] Bureau of Business Research, University of Texas, Howard County File.
[10] *West Texas Today*, XXXVII (May, 1956), 18–19.

than 26,000 in Howard County.[11] This trend continued, and in 1960 the population of the town was 31,230.[12] By 1950 the people of Big Spring had become more prosperous than many other Texans, for the median income of townspeople was $3,381, nearly $300.00 above the average for Texas.[13]

As more money became available, Big Spring residents approved new bonds for the construction of schools. In 1953 three new schools, including a $1,000,000 high school, were dedicated, and four years later ten elementary schools, a junior and a senior high school, and a junior college served the needs of the students of Big Spring.[14] Mainly as a result of this new construction, bonded indebtedness of the city and county rose to about $8,500,000 by 1957, and the total tax rate was $5.03 per $100.00.[15]

In 1957 Big Spring was still largely dependent on farming and retail trade for its income, although the petroleum industry, the Texas and Pacific shops, and Webb Air Force Base were extremely important in supporting the economy, especially during periods of drought. Oil production was less in Howard County than in some of the other counties under consideration, but it still was probably the greatest single source of steady income for the county.

In Sweetwater, as in Big Spring, there was a slight drop in population between 1930 and 1940, from 10,848 to 10,367 during the decade.[16] The depression was especially hard for Nolan County since there was no oil production whatsoever, and little industry other than the United States Gypsum Company. Retail sales totaled only $5,878,000 in 1939, and the county was dependent on agricultural production for its income.[17] Total wages from manufacturing concerns in the same year were $436,043.[18]

[11] *Seventeenth Census of the United States, 1950: Population*, I, 43–11.

[12] *Eighteenth Census of the United States, 1960: Population*, I, 21.

[13] This was true in all of the six counties under consideration (*Seventeenth Census of the United States, 1950: Population*, II, Part 43, pp. 43–127).

[14] *Fort Worth Star Telegram*, October 4, 1953 and November 17, 1957.

[15] Bureau of Business Research, University of Texas, Howard County File.

[16] *Sixteenth Census of the United States, 1940: Population*, I, 1059.

[17] *Ibid., Business*, I, 462.

[18] *Ibid., Manufacturing*, III, 984.

During the thirties cotton remained the chief crop on Nolan County farms. Peak production was reached in 1932 when 32,500 bales were ginned, and for the remainder of the decade about 10,000 bales were produced each year.[19] By 1940 there were 948 farms in the county, and the value of crops was only $994,528. In addition, about $130,000 was realized from the sale of dairy products, poultry, and eggs.[20] Ranching in Nolan County continued to be important, and sheep raising was growing more rapidly than the cattle industry. By 1940 all livestock, including 98,041 sheep, was valued at $1,285,855, and the industry had become one of the mainstays of agriculture in the county.[21]

There was not a great deal of improvement in the economic situation in Sweetwater and Nolan County before the late forties. As late as 1942 retail sales in Sweetwater were barely $7,000,000, but by 1948 they had reached $19,708,000. Little construction took place in the town during the depression, and by 1942 building permits still totaled only $67,500.[22] Between this date and 1950 construction gradually increased, and at the latter date permits for the year were valued at $1,808,720.[23] Although a measure of prosperity had returned to Sweetwater by 1950, not until after the discovery of oil in 1951 was there a great deal of business activity. Retail sales for 1952 were over $30,000,000, an almost direct result of the oil boom.[24] Approximately $200,000 a month was paid employees directly connected with the oil industry in Nolan County, and in addition, annual lease payments were about $600,000.[25] Income from the oil industry was a major factor in preventing a serious economic recession during the early fifties when the area was suffering from a drought.

The population of Sweetwater had risen to 13,619 by 1950 and

[19] Bureau of Business Research, University of Texas, Nolan County File.
[20] *Sixteenth Census of the United States, 1940: Agriculture*, II, 787.
[21] *Ibid., Agriculture*, I, 438.
[22] Bureau of Business Research, University of Texas, Nolan County File.
[23] *Sweetwater* (Texas) *Reporter*, January 4, 1951.
[24] *West Texas Today*, XXXVII (May, 1956), 18–19.
[25] *Sweetwater Reporter*, October 16, 1952.

leveled off at 13,914 in 1960.[26] Although the increase was slight, it indicated that the economic uncertainty that had caused a drop in population during the depression was at an end. The prosperity of the late forties was a natural result of the postwar expansion that was evident throughout the United States. That the development continued was partially due to the discovery and subsequent development of oil in the county.

Lamesa, although one of the smallest towns under consideration, demonstrated the most continuous growth. The population of Lamesa rose from 3,528 in 1930 to 6,038 in 1940, and ten years later it had reached 10,720.[27] The continual population growth occurred because the population movement to Dawson County began about ten years later than it had to other counties in the area, and as a result Dawson County was still going through the first stages of expansion when other areas were beginning to retrench.

The entire economy of Dawson County was based on agricultural production, especially cotton raising. During the late twenties cotton production averaged about 30,000 bales a year, and in both 1931 and 1932 more than 55,000 bales were ginned. Farmers suffered during the drought of the mid-thirties but by 1936 were again ginning 35,622 bales of cotton.[28] In 1940 the value of crops produced was $3,776,159, more than twice as much as in any other county under consideration. Besides crop production, Dawson County farmers and ranchers had livestock valued at $1,017,277 and sold dairy and poultry products for about $400,000 in 1940.[29] There was little business not connected with farming in the area surrounding Lamesa. The 1939 retail sales barely surpassed the value of crop pro-

[26] *Seventeenth Census of the United States, 1950: Population,* I, 43–12; *U.S. Census of Population, 1960: U.S. Summary,* p. 1–61.

[27] *Sixteenth Census of the United States, 1940: Population,* I, 1048; and *Seventeenth Census of the United States, 1950: Population,* I, 43–11.

[28] Almost no other crops were grown in Dawson County because farmers devoted nearly all their cultivated land to cotton, the best cash crop for the area (Texas, Agricultural Experiment Station, *Cotton Statistics of Texas,* 43–66).

[29] *Sixteenth Census of the United States, 1940: Agriculture,* II, 775.

duction and was $4,393,000.[30] There was almost no manufacturing in the county. The total value of manufactured goods in 1939 was $569,000, and wages were $56,922 for the 89 employees of manufacturing concerns.[31]

Beginning in 1945 Lamesa and Dawson County experienced a slight boom. Lamesa building permits, only $125,000 in 1945, increased rapidly and reached nearly $2,000,000 five years later. Retail sales in Lamesa were consistently above the $20,000,000 mark after 1950, and bank deposits rose from $10,329,306 in 1945 to just over $22,500,000 by 1950.[32] The discovery of the Spraberry sand and the subsequent oil activity contributed greatly to this expansion of business.

Agriculture also prospered during the forties and fifties except for the years of drought between 1951 and 1954. Cotton production continued to dominate farming, and between 85,000 and 150,000 bales were raised in good years of normal rainfall.[33] In 1950 some irrigation was started in the county, but since wells cost about $5,000 to drill, and an additional $5,000 was required to install a distribution system, few farmers were able to irrigate their farms. Even during years of drought, such as 1954, most cotton was grown on dry land, and the value of agricultural production in that year was about $15,000,000.[34] Four years later normal crop production was again possible, and gross receipts for crops were over $30,000,000.[35] Because Dawson County was a farming area it was only natural that the entire population would suffer to some degree when crops failed. However, the oil development of the early fifties helped take the edge from such periods of recession. By 1953 there were 265 producing

[30] *Ibid., Business,* I, 452.

[31] *Ibid., Manufacturing,* III, 983.

[32] Bureau of Business Research, University of Texas, Dawson County File.

[33] Texas, Agricultural Experiment Station, *Statistics of Texas Agriculture,* p. 365.

[34] *Fort Worth Star Telegram,* July 19, 1953.

[35] Cotton accounted for about $25,000,000 of the amount (Bureau of Business Research, University of Texas, Dawson County File).

wells in the county which brought in a continual income no matter what the weather might be.

During the two decades following 1930 Scurry County was largely a farming area, and Snyder, the county seat, was a small community catering to the needs of the farm population. There was no hint of the oil development that was to come, for only one small pool had been found in the county, and oil activity consisted of expansion of this field. Between 1930 and 1940 the population of Snyder rose from 3,008 to 3,815 as farmers in the area tried to continue crop production during the depression years.[36] The peak year of production was in 1932 when 52,000 bales of cotton were ginned, but the average for the decade was about 12,000 bales annually.[37] Crop production was up again in 1940, and in that year the value of crops harvested was $1,514,643. At the same time livestock worth $1,183,310 was grazed on farms and ranches, and nearly $700,000 was received from the sale of dairy and poultry products.[38] Manufactured products in 1940 were valued at only $435,766, and retail trade was less than $3,000,000.[39] Despite the lack of diversification in the economy of the county, the people were fairly prosperous when, in the late forties, the discovery of oil in the Emil Schattel and Winston wells made Snyder a boom town overnight.

Within two years of the discovery of oil in November 1948, it was difficult to recognize Snyder as the same town. From a town of about 4,200 people, it became a bustling small city of nearly 20,000 as oil crews, speculators, and oil service organizations swarmed to the community.[40] At the time of the discovery one small hotel and four tourist courts, most of them old, provided accommodations for travelers. In 1950 eleven courts and four hotels had 628 rooms for rent. So difficult was it to find rooms that 3,200 trailer houses moved

---

[36] *Sixteenth Census of the United States, 1940: Population,* I, 1059.

[37] Texas, Agricultural Experiment Station, *Cotton Statistics of Texas,* pp. 10–60.

[38] *Sixteenth Census of the United States, 1940: Agriculture,* II, 789.

[39] *Ibid., Manufacturing,* III, 984; and *Ibid., Business,* I, 464.

[40] *World Oil,* CXXXII (March, 1951), 202.

to the town.[41] People were found sleeping in wrecked cars and under highway bridges, and about 600 people commuted from Sweetwater, forty miles away.[42]

All aspects of the business life prospered during 1949 and 1950. Bank deposits in the one bank rose from $2,000,000 to over $16,000,000 by 1950, and a bank organized in 1949 had $5,600,000 on deposit by 1950.[43] Tax evaluations were estimated to be less than $6,000,000 in 1948; by 1949 they had risen to $35,000,000 and in 1953 were $120,000,000.[44] Construction showed the effects of the boom also as the amount of building permits rose from $315,000 in 1948 to $2,571,240 the following year.[45]

The tremendous influx of people to Snyder presented a variety of problems for the small community. The need for hospitals and health facilities, restaurants, retail outlets, and schools affected both the town government and the ordinary citizen. In 1949 it became necessary to pass an ordinance requiring that all trailers be connected to a sewer line. Since there were many areas within the city limits which had no sewers, a $1,150,000 bond issue was voted to increase the capacity of the existing sewage disposal plant and to extend water and sewer mains.[46]

Before the oil boom hit, there were 962 students in the Snyder school system, and school property was valued at $500,000. By 1952, 3,104 pupils attended school in the city, and school property was worth $5,500,000.[47] Oil companies aided in building the school system in two ways. When it became obvious that an immediate solution to the need for schools had to be found, eleven oil companies offered to advance any funds needed and to let the amount stand as

---

[41] *Ibid.*; and *West Texas Today*, XXXI (May, 1950), 26.

[42] *Fort Worth Star Telegram*, December 11, 1949.

[43] These deposits were the result of new accounts opened by new residents (*Abilene* [Texas] *Reporter News*, August 23, 1953).

[44] *Ibid.*

[45] *Dallas Morning News*, January 8, 1950.

[46] Eventually the number of trailers allowed in the town was limited (*West Texas Today*, XXXI [May, 1950], 7).

[47] *Abilene Reporter News*, August 23, 1953.

a credit against future taxes.[48] Also, oil companies supported the Snyder schools after the tax credits had been paid. The state per capita apportionment for schools was only 17.4 per cent of the total school income.[49] Oil companies paid 68.6 per cent, and royalty owners were responsible for 10.6 per cent.[50]

The population movement to Snyder was not all temporary. In 1950 there were 12,010 people in the town, and in 1957 the population was estimated to be 17,926.[51] Retail sales in the city remained above the $30,000,000 level after the oil boom, and by 1958 tax evaluations had risen to $137,104,816. At that date the total employment in the county was 10,065, and only 425 people were unemployed.[52]

Agriculture, although overshadowed, was not completely supplanted by the oil industry, and during the boom both ranching and farming prospered. In 1957 agricultural production of the county was valued at $15,234,595, with cotton still the principal crop. At that time there were 208,000 acres of land in cultivation on Scurry County farms, but only 3,500 acres of this amount were under irrigation because irrigation was too expensive for many farmers to put down wells.[53] By 1957 Snyder had settled down to become a considerably quieter city than it had been in 1949, but the changes made during the period of the boom were permanent. Snyder had become an oil town, and its future depended primarily on the petroleum industry.

The development of Midland was similar to, though not as sudden as, that of Snyder. Since Midland early became the center for representatives of oil companies, as long as there was drilling in the Permian Basin, there was little chance that the city would cease to grow. Although the activity in the oil fields was not great during the depression, Midland grew in population from 5,484 in 1930 to 9,352

[48] *World Oil*, CXXXII (March, 1951), 203.
[49] *Abilene Reporter News*, August 23, 1953; and *Dallas Morning News*, October 14, 1953.
[50] *Seventeenth Census of the United States, 1950: Population*, I, 43–12.
[51] *Ibid.*
[52] Bureau of Business Research, University of Texas, Scurry County File.
[53] *Ibid.*

ten years later.[54] The growth of the city after 1940 was almost phenomenal, for the population in 1950 was 21,713, and by 1960 had
reached 62,625.[55]

The constantly increasing population of Midland was almost entirely the result of oil activity in the surrounding counties. Agriculture, other than ranching, was never very important in Midland
County. In 1940 the total value of crops was only $396,583, and
nearly $200,000 was realized from the sale of dairy and poultry
products. At the same time the value of livestock was $1,239,130 in
Midland County.[56] During the forties and fifties crop production continued to decrease. By 1949 there were only 70,000 acres being
cultivated in the county, about 4,500 of which were irrigated.[57]
Ranching continued to be important, and in 1949 there were 25,000
cattle and 30,000 sheep on ranches in the county.

With the movement of oil companies and oil-well supply organizations to Midland in 1928, the city became basically dependent on the
petroleum industry. Typical of the large companies with offices in
Midland was Shell Oil Corporation. Shell entered into leasing activities in West Texas in 1924 and in 1935 established an office in
Midland. By 1948 the company had 275 employees in the city and
was preparing to take over six floors of the Petroleum Building for
its district headquarters. Another major company, Humble Oil and
Refining, in 1952 reported that it planned to spend approximately
$55,000,000 during 1952 in the West Texas–New Mexico Division,
administered from the district office at Midland.[58] These large companies were typical of the concerns that made Midland a growing
and prosperous city on the West Texas plains.

Following the discovery of oil in Midland County in 1945 and the

[54] *Sixteenth Census of the United States, 1940: Population,* I.

[55] *Seventeenth Census of the United States, 1950: Population,* I, 43–12; and
Eighteenth Census of the United States, 1960: Population, I, 23.

[56] Crop production fell drastically during the depression years (*Sixteenth
Census of the United States, 1940: Agriculture,* II, 785).

[57] Midland County Agent, letter to Bureau of Business Research, University
of Texas, February 17, 1950.

[58] *Midland* (Texas) *Reporter Telegram,* March 8, 1952.

renewed drilling activity in all of the Permian Basin after the war, Midland grew rapidly. As a result, retail sales, which had been $5,935,000 in 1940, reached $25,753,000 in 1948, and in 1953 were $63,814,000.[59] Other businesses made corresponding gains. Building permits increased from $1,544,805 in 1945 to more than $30,000,000 in 1958. Bank deposits rose from $22,570,177 in 1945 to $113,885,604 in 1958.[60] This development of the economy was basically the result of the presence of 650 major and independent oil companies, which, with their employees, contributed greatly to the business life of the community.

Ector County, and its county seat, Odessa, were even more dependent on oil production than was Midland. Ector County had the largest petroleum production in the Permian Basin and also housed the greatest number of industries related to petroleum. Scene of the first important discoveries in the Permian Basin, Ector County continued to grow throughout this period. The population of the county was concentrated in Odessa, which grew from 2,407 to 9,573 residents between 1930 and 1940.[61] The population growth after 1940 was even greater, for there was much more oil activity in the area. In 1950 the population of Odessa was 29,495 and by 1960 had reached 80,338.[62]

This population growth was entirely the result of oil production and a little manufacturing, mostly connected with the petroleum industry. In 1940 production of crops in Ector County brought a little more than $10,000, and at that time livestock was valued at $393,650.[63] From that date on agricultural production decreased and the industry virtually disappeared. Manufacturing in 1940 produced goods valued at $954,544, and accounted for $132,981 in wages.[64]

[59] *Sixteenth Census of the United States, 1940: Business*, I, 460; and *West Texas Today*, XXXVII (May, 1956), 18–19.

[60] Bureau of Business Research, University of Texas, Midland County File.

[61] *Sixteenth Census of the United States, 1940: Population*, I, 1059.

[62] *Seventeenth Census of the United States, 1950: Population*, I, 43–12; and *Eighteenth Census of the United States, 1960: Population*, I, 83.

[63] *Sixteenth Census of the United States, 1940: Agriculture*, II, 776.

[64] *Ibid., Manufacturing*, III, 983.

Industry countered the loss in agricultural income through the development of sulphur plants, natural gasoline installations, and the General Tire and Rubber Company's factory.

The postwar boom in Odessa caused prices to soar and business to grow. From 1945 on the city was in an almost continuous state of rapid growth, and consequently there was a shortage of low-cost housing. A large number of such homes were rushed to completion, and the city also provided temporary quarters for new residents in trailer houses.[65] Store and office space was also at a premium. The construction of a large number of new homes and buildings caused building permits to rise from $2,300,000 in 1946 to $27,962,126 for 1957.[66]

A great variety of building was done during this period. In 1950 the eight-story Lincoln Hotel was begun after citizens formed the Civic Hotel Corporation and agreed to subscribe half of the $1,200,000 cost.[67] In 1953 Phillips Petroleum began a $1,000,000 office building; two years later a municipal coliseum costing about $600,000 and a Medical Center addition costing $750,000 were completed; and in 1957 voters approved a $4,358,584 school bond issue.[68] These were only a few representative examples of the building that took place in Odessa.

A look at almost any business activity showed the same type of growth. Bank deposits increased 600 per cent between 1945 and 1958, retail sales more than doubled from the late forties to 1954, and tax evaluations rose from $28,552,130 in 1946 to $47,065,-165 only three years later.[69] Odessa, like Midland, was a shipping and supply center for a large area. Gross sales of oil-field equipment and servicing organizations in Odessa annually totaled more than $200,000,000.[70] Added to this were the profits from the sale of oil

[65] *West Texas Today*, XXVIII (August, 1947), 7.
[66] *Dallas Morning News*, October 18, 1958.
[67] *Ibid.*, July 3, 1950.
[68] *Fort Worth Star Telegram*, July 5, 1953; *El Paso* (Texas) *Times*, January 7, 1955; and *Odessa* (Texas) *American*, May 19, 1957 and July 14, 1958.
[69] Bureau of Business Research, University of Texas, Ector County File; and *Dallas Morning News*, October 23, 1949.
[70] *Odessa American*, July 18, 1957.

and gas, salaries paid drilling crews, value of products from petroleum-connected industries, and lease and royalty payments. All this activity gave the full picture of the impact of the oil industry on Odessa and Ector County.

The population of the six cities and counties under consideration in this study rose from 8,837 in 1900 to 156,276 by 1950 and reached 257,368 by 1960; city population, negligible in 1900, was 104,827 in 1950 and 214,395 in 1960.[71] Although a rural area dependent on farming for revenue until after 1930, by 1960 West Texas had become a section where most of the population lived in small cities, and farming was, in all but one county, a secondary source of income.

The general pattern of growth indicated that the economic picture in West Texas would remain relatively unchanged as far as the importance of particular industries was concerned. Oil and oil-connected industries played such a crucial role in the overall financial picture that they completely dominated other industrial interests. In 1958 manufacturing establishments in the six-county area paid $23,494,000 in wages and added $78,061,000 to the value of the raw materials.[72] During 1960 the total value of mineral products produced was $468,257,329.[73] With the possible exceptions of

[71] *Twelfth Census of the United States, 1900: Population,* I; *Seventeenth Census of the United States, 1950: Population,* I; and *Eighteenth Census of the United States, 1960: Population,* I, 21–23.

[72] It should also be noted that much of this total value is in oil-connected industries. A breakdown by counties shows that most of the manufacturing was done in Ector, Nolan, and Howard counties, each of which contributed over $20,000,000 to the total (*United States Census of Manufacturing,* 1958, III: Area Statistics, pp. 42–6, to 42–8).

[73] Production of oil and natural gas in the area was:

County	Crude oil (1000's bbls)	Natural Gas (mil c/f)
Howard	12,723	2,238
Midland	14,102	95,124
Nolan	5,162	6,784
Scurry	29,786	13,110
Dawson	6,459	1,727
Ector	56,769	79,889

Value of all mineral products by county was: Dawson, $20,063,513; Ector,

Howard and Nolan counties, which have more diversified economies, the counties in the area under consideration are likely to remain largely dependent on the oil industry.

Developments in West Texas were not merely the result of a growing population in Texas or of a general westward movement in the state. The semiarid soil of West Texas had little to offer in the way of inducement to bring people out on the plains. Special circumstances and a number of factors caused the rise of the city in West Texas.

As immigrants moved into the area during the eighteen-seventies, they settled along creeks. Even to these early settlers it was obvious that the procurement of water was a major problem of life on the plains of Texas. The second important factor involved in the establishment of towns was transportation. The Texas and Pacific Railroad, crossing the plains in 1881 and 1882, passed within a few miles of Sweetwater, and the town promptly removed to the track site. The road went through Big Spring, and Midland and Odessa were actually first established as depots and section houses for the line.

The towns that developed first and most rapidly were those with both water and transportation facilities. Thus Snyder and Lamesa, both of which were somewhat isolated, did not grow quickly. The first period of urban growth in West Texas coincided with the dominance of ranching in the area, and early towns were mostly in areas where the livestock industry was important. Midland and Odessa, situated in counties where the industry got a later start, grew more slowly at first.

The early years of development were a testing period during which it was determined whether or not the towns could continue to exist in the forbidding climate of West Texas. Those which managed to survive grew slowly until farming entered the economic picture of the region. Between 1910 and 1925 occurred a second major time of development. During these years farming, given impetus by un-

---

$210,047,973; Howard, $42,414,802; Midland, $65,214,790; Nolan, $26,821,-301; Scurry, $103,695,050 (U.S., Bureau of Mines, *Minerals Yearbook*, 1962, III: Area Reports, pp. 1009–1010, 1023–1026).

usually good weather and the wartime markets and prices, became the main occupation in West Texas. Once again, transportation was a prime concern, and water was necessary for continued growth.

With the period of falling prices in the late twenties and the drought and depression years of the thirties, there was not much urban change in the area under consideration. Not until the first impact of the oil industry and the general upswing of business following World War II did the towns grow a great deal. During this period only two small cities, Midland and Odessa, showed signs of substantial growth. Only these two, of the six under consideration, were almost completely dependent on oil by the thirties. Since some oil activity in the area continued throughout the depression decade, they were little affected by the economic downswing. At that time the future of urban development in West Texas could be seen in these two communities.

The last period of great development came in the late forties and early fifties when the rise of cities took place as the result of the discovery of oil in the Permian Basin. Transportation, water, agriculture, and oil have each played a part in the increase of population and in the improvement of the economy in central West Texas. Without transportation and water the towns could not have existed, without agriculture they could not have grown, and without oil they could never have become as large as they did.

Each of these factors and the importance each had for a particular city determined to a large extent the ultimate size of that community. It was these factors that caused some towns not to develop at all. Borden County was a large producer of oil, but Gail, the county seat, had neither adequate transportation facilities nor sufficient water supplies or agricultural development to make it grow. The same situation was to be found in other towns in the general area, such as Kermit in Winkler County, Seminole in Gaines County, and Colorado City in Mitchell County.

The factors involved in the growth of towns in this region also play an important part in the future of the section. In this respect petroleum and water are of primary importance. The largest of the cities, Odessa and Midland, are completely dependent on oil for their continued development. Vast oil reserves have already been uncovered in the Permian Basin, and new techniques of secondary recovery will probably increase these reserves. Under the proration plans of the Texas Railroad Commission the area is assured many years of oil production, and this in turn means that industry, which is basically dependent on petroleum, can continue to develop.

These larger cities are in an extremely precarious position, however, for although oil will be produced into the foreseeable future, the day will inevitably arrive when there is no more petroleum available. When that day comes, it will be the cities with a diversified economy, the ones that have agriculture or other industries to fall back on, which will survive. Oil, which has been a blessing to West Texas, could also be its eventual downfall.

Urbanization in this area is also dangerous because of the critical water problem. By 1960 the population of the cities in West Texas had risen to a point that reasonably demanded some long-range planning in order to assure an adequate and permanent supply of water. Since the possibility of replenishing the underground table was at best questionable, some other source of supply appeared the more likely solution to the problem. By far the most workable and financially sound program was the Colorado River project. Financed by the sale of bonds and controlled by the members of the water district, it proved to be both economically sound and an adequate source of water for the cooperating cities.

Since very few sites exist in West Texas for the construction of dams capable of impounding large quantities of water, it is essential that they be utilized and that the construction of a large number of small reservoirs not be allowed. Another factor supporting this contention is the fact that the rate of evaporation in the area is high, and the total amount of surface exposed would be less in one large lake than in many small reservoirs.

Two problems exist that make any sensible water program difficult to carry out. First, there is the shortsightedness of individuals and government officials in the area. There has been almost no thought of conservation of existing supply sources, and waste of water by farmers who have irrigation wells is still allowed. Second is the provincialism of many people in the area which expresses itself in a fear of federal control. Although the CRMWD was carried out by local funds entirely, this might not be possible in all cases, and matching funds from the United States government might not only be necessary but preferable. Opposition to the use of such funds and distaste for the accompanying regulations and controls had, as late as 1959, prevented other similar programs from making any headway.

The problem of obtaining a sufficient water supply has become greater as the population of West Texas has grown, and it will continue to become greater in the future. The influx of people and the beginning of industry after the discovery of oil has intensified the problem and has made it imperative that a solution be found if the region is to continue as a populated area. What the scientific advances of the future may hold can not be predicted. Perhaps the use of atomic power to convert and transport sea water to the area will prove feasible, or possibly some other technological advance will provide a solution, but until that time comes a more honest and realistic attitude toward the problem should be adopted by the people most closely connected with it, the residents of West Texas. If such an attitude is not taken, it may very well mean that the urbanization of central West Texas will eventually leave in its wake a series of ghost towns on the prairies.

APPENDIX I[1]

Political Climate of Central West Texas

Political developments of at least enough importance to merit mention have taken place in this area of Texas during the past few years. Whether or not they are directly related to either urbanization or industrialization is impossible to determine without further investigation of an entirely different nature, but political tendencies in the area under consideration have been toward political conservatism. Barometers of political change in Texas are difficult to determine at best because of the dominant role of the Democratic Party and the influence of local issues in campaigns which make it hard to evaluate changes in a state of this size. In an attempt to indicate the nature of political feeling in this area, I have taken a few election returns that offer a fairly clear-cut choice between what pass for liberals and conservatives in Texas.

Gubernatorial Election, 1954

County	Shivers(D) (conservative)	Ralph Yarborough(D) (liberal)
Dawson	1706	1377
Ector	4288	3505
Howard	2538	3225
Midland	4316	2303
Scurry	1600	2014
Nolan	1726	2368

Presidential and Senatorial Elections, 1960

County	Kennedy(D)	Nixon(R)	Johnson(D)	Tower(R)
Dawson	2063	2161	2549	1590
Ector	8976	10,945	9204	9310
Howard	4844	3404	5649	2600
Midland	5842	11,343	6702	9238
Nolan	3247	2421	3762	1786
Scurry	3015	2248	3343	1772

[1] Figures included here are taken from the *Texas Almanac*, 1955–1966.

First Democratic Primary, 1962, Gubernatorial Election

County	Connally (conservative)	Walker (extreme conservative)	Don Yarborough (liberal)
Dawson	540	130	408
Ector	1984	2590	2110
Howard	1010	384	2330
Midland	2173	1579	790
Nolan	994	490	1018
Scurry	616	288	1173

Second Democratic Primary, 1962

County	Connally (conservative)	Don Yarborough (liberal)
Dawson	1121	1015
Ector	2821	3555
Howard	1433	2894
Midland	3598	2043
Nolan	1607	2246
Scurry	1305	2498

General Election, 1962, Gubernatorial Election

County	Connally (D)	Cox (R) (conservative)
Dawson	1503	1404
Ector	5720	9017
Howard	2981	2239
Midland	4578	9066
Nolan	2539	1409
Scurry	1684	1453

Presidential Election, 1964

County	Johnson (D)	Goldwater (R)
Dawson	3171	1691
Ector	10,826	11,497
Howard	6083	3272
Midland	8684	11,906
Nolan	3540	1610
Scurry	3381	1741

It would be risky to make substantial deductions from these figures; however, some generalizations can be attempted. The vote in 1954 on a fairly clear-cut choice seems to indicate that there was not a substantial division along conservative-liberal lines, although the tendency was toward the conservative side. Shivers' victory in 1954 reflects the general pattern in the state. By 1960 the Republican candidate carried the two largest counties in the region and ran well in all others. Perhaps most significant were the three elections in 1962. The sizable vote in some counties in the first primary for the very conservative General Edwin Walker indicates the degree of conservatism in those areas. A surprising shift took place in the second primary when the liberal candidate got substantial support in areas where he had little before. This resulted from a campaign to vote for Yarborough in the primary on the assumption that he would be easier to defeat in the general election than Connally. The figures for the general election show that many so-called Democrats shifted to the Republican column at that time. In the 1964 presidential race, Goldwater not only carried the two largest counties, but also ran better in this area than he did nationally. Indeed, the essentially conservative Texas Republican Party finds much of its strength in West Texas.

Dr. Murray Clark Havens, Professor of Political Science at The University of Texas, read a paper at the 1964 Southwest Social Science Meeting in which he studied "The Impact of Right Wing Groups in Selected Texas Cities." Both Midland and Odessa were among the cities studied. Of the urban areas investigated, Havens found that only in Odessa had the John Birch Society been able to maintain its dominance for a considerable length of time. He shows that while Odessa, which has good labor organization and a tradition of political liberalism, seemed less likely to become Birch-dominated than did Midland, no anti-Birch leadership developed there. In Midland, however, a small group created an effective defensive alignment. Professor Havens points out that when traditional leadership loses touch with its people and with political reality, serious inroads can be made in the community by such an organization as the John Birch Society. This may explain why, in the area under consideration, it was only in the larger cities that the John Birch Society had much effect. That this and similar organizations have had some effect on politics in West Texas is certainly true.

APPENDIX II

Figures included here are taken from U.S., Department of Commerce, Bureau of the Census, *Twelfth* through *Fifteenth Census of the United States, 1900–1930: Agriculture.*

A. Data on Farming, 1900–1930

County	Date	Number Farms and Ranches	Number Tenants	Improved Acreage	Value Land (per acre)	Value Crops (dollars)	Value Machinery
HOWARD	1900	130	20	5,835	1.22	124,093	15,860
	1910	819	425	84,799	11.25	299,810	153,068
	1920	422	167	65,363	16.64	2,177,089	188,887
	1930	1,194	808	145,555	23.50	2,017,818	486,309
NOLAN	1900	293	60	179,640	2.28	144,360	22,250
	1910	1,160	634	93,296	14.98	795,431	191,904
	1920	1,015	528	114,621	18.88	5,072,471	390,694
	1930	1,154	665	134,217	26.90	2,205,926	548,804
SCURRY	1900	586	134	38,144	1.78	334,379	64,300
	1910	1,424	709	144,642	16.62	639,913	254,642
	1920	1,077	566	140,886	25.07	5,677,857	471,635
	1930	1,564	201	202,510	25.30	2,048,151	674,554
MIDLAND	1900	73	8	897	0.77	214,822*	9,365
	1910	128	52	16,166	8.87	44,407	40,205
	1920	133	47	14,899	9.06	312,964	127,095
	1930	361	104	70,923	14.20	813,161	140,905
ECTOR	1900	25	14	92	0.67	69,681*	18,110
	1910	84	11	4,796	6.72	19,753	31,950
	1920	55	7	10,451	7.09	49,821	42,975
	1930	69	27	2,824	8.72	39,127	52,945
DAWSON	1900	5	1	35	1.09	-----	2,220
	1910	330	106	42,631	18.21	70,932	55,710
	1920	574	195	61,074	24.16	2,928,075	194,754
	1930	2,218	978	172,917	31.08	3,990,222	958,471

* These figures from the 1900 U.S. Census are obviously inaccurate

B. Agricultural Production, 1900–1930

County	Date	Cotton (bales)	Wheat (bushels)	Sorghum (bushels)	Corn (bushels)	Cattle (number)	Sheep (number)
HOWARD	1900	199	......	......	4,450	21,928	5,424
	1910	22,197	1,800	102,740	6,866	32,545	280
	1920	7,349	8,816	334,706	35,129	12,065	11,272
	1930	17,793	......	161,696	3,496	19,749	5,205
NOLAN	1900	1,830	4,450	......	56,100	23,998	4,755
	1910	6,372	5	225,404	15,480	15,889	7,454
	1920	18,124	54,300	669,829	43,591	13,540	18,529
	1930	10,068	2,635	186,016	14,423	17,856	41,181
SCURRY	1900	2,860	6,220	......	75,680	23,823	2,999
	1910	4,802	......	301,923	16,549	24,837	972
	1920	18,981	64,206	812,502	51,417	14,433	2,978
	1930	18,325	6,780	162,074	3,765	20,288	17,738
MIDLAND	1900	......	......	......	......	14,096	2,252
	1910	1,755	......	21,292	3,415	28,796	31
	1920	951	......	......	1,398	54,782	......
	1930	6,388	......	41,588	1,075	36,412	808
ECTOR	1900	......	......	......	......	21,285	......
	1910	30	......	15,740	2,224	23,765	5
	1920	54	......	......	......	11,060	......
	1930	257	......	6,700	1,645	15,995	1,172
DAWSON	1900	......	......	......	......	9,900	......
	1910	207	......	48,693	17,911	5,729	413
	1920	9,447	1,710	476,357	112,305	18,694	3,479
	1930	33,978	......	182,640	3,622	16,352	1,006

APPENDIX III[1]

Permian Basin Oil and Gas, 1963 Statistics

Producing reservoirs (producing crude oil and/or natural gas and/ or gas-liquid)	2,795
Producing wells (gas, crude, or condensate)	86,366
Average daily production (crude oil and natural gas liquids)	1,515,862 bbls.
Total petroleum liquid production (crude oil and natural gas liquids)	553,289,626 bbls.
Cumulative production of all petroleum- liquid through 1963	10,154,450,611 bbls.
Estimated proven reserves of natural gas liquid	670,600,000 bbls.
Estimated proven reserves of crude oil	6,658,000,000 bbls.
Estimated proven reserves of natural gas	27,711,000,000,000 cu. ft.
Natural gas production	1,804,849,052,000 cu. ft.

[1] U.S., Bureau of Mines, *Minerals Yearbook, 1963.*

SOURCES CONSULTED

UNITED STATES PUBLICATIONS

Adams, George I. *Oil and Gas Fields of the Western Interior and Northern Texas Coal Measures and of the Upper Cretaceous and Tertiary of the Western Gulf Coast.* United States Geological Survey Bulletin Number 184. Washington: Government Printing Office, 1901.

Hill, Robert T. *The Present Condition of Knowledge of the Geology of Texas.* United States Geological Survey Bulletin Number 45. Washington: Government Printing Office, 1887.

Hoots, H. W. *Geology of a Part of Western Texas and Southeastern New Mexico: With a Special Reference to Salt and Potash.* United States Geological Survey Bulletin Number 780. Washington: Government Printing Office, 1926.

Livingston, Penn, and Robert R. Bennett. *Geology and Ground Water Resources of the Big Spring Area, Texas.* Water Supply Paper 913. Washington: Government Printing Office, 1944.

Marcy, Randolph B. *Exploration of the Red River of Louisiana in the Year 1952.* House of Representatives, 33rd Cong., 1st sess. Exec. Doc. Washington: Government Printing Office, 1854.

Mineral Resources of the United States, 1901, 1913, 1926–1931.

Richardson, George Burr. "Petroleum Near Dayton, New Mexico," in *Contributions to Economic Geology in 1912,* Part II: *Mineral Fuels.* Washington: Government Printing Office, 1913.

———. "Salt, Gypsum and Petroleum in Trans-Pecos Texas," in *Contributions to Economic Geology in 1904.* Washington: Government Printing Office, 1905.

U. S. Bureau of Mines. *Minerals Yearbook, 1962.* Washington, D.C.: Government Printing Office, 1963.

———. *Minerals Yearbook, 1963.* Washington, D.C.: Government Printing Office, 1964.

U. S. Congress. Senate. Sen. Doc. 64, 31st Cong., 1st sess., 1851.

———. Sen. Doc. 45, 52nd Cong., 1st sess., 1891.

U. S. Department of Agriculture. *Yearbook of the United States Department of Agriculture, 1900.* Washington: Government Printing Office, 1891.

U. S. Department of Commerce. Bureau of the Census. *Tenth* through *Eighteenth Census of the United States,* 1880–1960.

White, Charles A. *The Texas Permian and Its Mesozoic Types of Fossils.* United States Geological Survey Bulletin Number 77. Washington: Government Printing Office, 1891.

TEXAS STATE PUBLICATIONS AND AGENCY FILES

Bently, W. P. *The Geology of Coke County.* Austin: State Printer, 1918.
Broadhurst, W. L., *et al. Public Water Supplies in Western Texas.* Austin: State Printer, 1949.
Buechel, F. A. *Farm Cash Income in Texas, 1927–1936.* Austin: State Printer, 1936.
Buckley, S. B. *First Annual Report of the Geological and Agricultural Survey of Texas.* Houston: State Printer, 1874.
Bureau of Business Research, University of Texas. *Economic Surveys of Dawson, Ector, Howard, Midland, Nolan and Scurry Counties.* Austin: University of Texas Press, 1949.
———. Austin, Texas. Files on Dawson, Ector, Howard, Midland, Nolan, and Scurry Counties.
Dumble, Edwin T. *First Report of Progress of the Geological and Mineralogical Survey of Texas.* Austin: State Printer, 1889.
Knowles, D. B. *Ground-Water Resources of Ector County, Texas.* Texas State Board of Water Engineers Bulletin 5210. Austin: State Printer, 1952.
Liddle, R. A. *The Marathon Fold and Its Influence on Petroleum Accumulation.* Austin: State Printer, 1918.
Richardson, George Burr. *Report of a Reconnaissance in Trans-Pecos Texas, North of the Texas and Pacific Railway.* Austin: State Printer, 1904.
Texas. Agricultural Experiment Station. *Calibration of Cotton Planting Mechanisms.* College Station: Texas Agricultural and Mechanical College Press, 1936.
———. *Commercial Fertilizers in 1924–1925.* College Station: Texas Agricultural and Mechanical College Press, 1925.
———. *Commercial Fertilizers in 1924–1925 and Their Use.* College Station: Texas Agricultural and Mechanical College Press, 1929.
———. *The Effect of Spacing on the Yield of Cotton.* College Station: Texas Agricultural and Mechanical College Press, 1926.
———. *Farm Mortgage Financing in Texas.* College Station: Texas Agricultural and Mechanical College Press, 1925.

———. *Large Scale Cotton Production in Texas.* College Station: Texas Agricultural and Mechanical College Press, 1927.

———. *Mechanical Harvesting of Cotton.* College Station: Texas Agricultural and Mechanical College Press, 1932.

———. *Mechanical Harvesting of Cotton in Northwest Texas.* College Station: Texas Agricultural and Mechanical College Press, 1928.

———. *Mechanized Production of Cotton in Texas.* College Station: Texas Agricultural and Mechanical College Press, 1948.

———. *Short-Term Farm Credit in Texas.* College Station: Texas Agricultural and Mechanical College Press, 1927.

———. *The Soils of Texas.* College Station: Texas Agricultural and Mechanical College Press, 1931.

———. *Statistics of Texas Agriculture.* College Station: Texas Agricultural and Mechanical College Press, 1937.

———. *Statistics of Texas Agriculture.* College Station: Texas Agricultural and Mechanical College Press, 1953.

———. *Sudan Grass for Hay, Seed and Pasture.* College Station: Texas Agricultural and Mechanical College Press, 1929.

Texas. Commissioner of the General Land Office. *Biennial Report of the Commissioner of the General Land Office of Texas,* 1880–1922. Austin: State Printer, 1883–1922.

Texas. Department of Agriculture. *Annual Report of the Commissioner of Agriculture, 1908–1954.* Austin: State Printer, 1909–1955.

———. *Annual Report of the Agricultural Bureau of the Department of Agriculture, Insurance, Statistics, and History.* Austin: State Printer, 1889–1897.

———. *Year Book, 1908.* Austin: State Printer, 1909.

———. *Year Book, 1909.* Austin: State Printer, 1910.

Texas. State Archives. Austin, Texas. Manuscript Census of Texas, 1880.

———. Records Division. Land Lease Receipts of the General Land Office of Texas, 1888–1900.

———. Records Division. Tax Assessor's Rolls for Dawson, Ector, Howard, Midland, Nolan, and Scurry Counties.

Texas. State Board of Water Engineers. Austin, Texas. Canadian River Water District File.

———. Colorado River Municipal Water District File.

———. Files of Dawson, Ector, Howard, Midland, Nolan, and Scurry Counties.

---

174   *The City Moves West*

BOOKS

American Association of Petroleum Geologists. *Structure of Typical American Oil Fields.* 2 Vols. Tulsa, Oklahoma: American Association of Petroleum Geologists, 1929.

Barrett, Velma, and Hazel Oliver. *Odessa: City of Dreams, A Miracle of the Texas Prairies.* San Antonio, Texas: The Naylor Company, 1952.

Bizzell, William Bennett. *Rural Texas.* New York: Macmillan Co., 1924.

Cotten, Kathryn. *Saga of Scurry.* San Antonio, Texas: The Naylor Company, 1957.

Cox, James. *Historical and Biographical Record of the Cattle Industry and the Cattlemen of Texas and Adjacent Territory.* St. Louis: Woodward and Tierman, 1895.

Dale, Edward Everett. *The Range Cattle Industry.* Norman: University of Oklahoma Press, 1930.

Fancher, George H., et al. *The Oil Resources of Texas.* Austin: Texas Petroleum Research Committee, 1954.

Gammel, H. P. N., ed. *The Laws of Texas, 1822–1897.* 10 Vols. Austin: The Gammel Book Company, 1898.

Glass, Mrs. George. *History of Midland.* Midland: n.p., n.d.

Herald, Frank A., ed. *Occurrence of Oil and Gas in West Texas.* Austin: University of Texas Press, 1957.

Hill, James. *The End of the Cattle Trail.* New York: Macmillan Co., 1920.

Holden, William Curry. *Alkali Trails, or Social and Economic Movements of the Texas Frontier, 1846–1900.* Dallas: The Southwest Press, 1930.

Hunter, J. Marvin, ed. and comp. *The Trail Drivers of Texas,* 2nd ed., rev. Nashville: Cokebury Press, 1925.

Hutto, John R. *Howard County in the Making.* Big Spring: Jordan's, 1938.

Johnson, Elmer H. *The Basis of the Commercial and Industrial Development of Texas.* Austin: University of Texas Press, 1933.

Midland REPORTER. Midland: *Midland* REPORTER, 1912.

Moore, Raymond G. *Historical Geology.* New York: McGraw-Hill, 1933.

Neill, Raymond F. *History of Dawson County.* Lamesa, Texas: Mulberry Printing Co., 1953.

Nordyke, Lewis, *Great Roundup, the Story of Texas and Southwestern Cowmen.* New York: William Morrow, 1955.

Osgood, Ernest Staples. *The Day of the Cattlemen.* Chicago: University of Chicago Press, 1929.

Philips, Shine. *Big Spring, The Casual Biography of a Prairie Town.* New York: Prentice-Hall, 1942.

Richardson, Rupert Norval. *Texas, The Lone Star State.* New York: Prentice-Hall, 1943.

Rister, Carl Coke. *Fort Griffin on the Texas Frontier.* Norman: University of Oklahoma Press, 1956.

———. *Oil! Titan of the Southwest.* Norman: University of Oklahoma Press, 1949.

Schuchert, Charles, and Carl O. Dunbar. *Outlines of Historical Geology.* 4th ed. New York: John Wiley and Sons, 1941.

Southwestern Immigration Company. *Texas: Her Resources and Capabilities.* New York: E. D. Slater, 1881.

Tait, Samuel W. *The Wildcatters, An Informal History of Oil Hunting in America.* Princeton, New Jersey: Princeton University Press, 1946.

Wallis, George A. *Cattle Kings of the Staked Plains.* Dallas: The American Guild Press, 1957.

Webb, Walter Prescott. *The Texas Rangers, A Century of Frontier Defense.* New York: Houghton Mifflin, 1935.

White, E. V., and William E. Leonard. *Studies in Farm Tenancy in Texas.* Austin: University of Texas Press, 1915.

Wortham, Louis J. *A History of Texas.* 5 Vols. Fort Worth: Clark Press, 1924.

UNPUBLISHED THESES

Bradford, Louise. "A History of Nolan County, Texas." Master's Thesis, University of Texas, 1934.

Horton, Finas Wade. "A History of Ector County, Texas." Master's Thesis, University of Texas, 1950.

Huff, Millicent Seay. "A Study of Work Done By Texas Railroad Companies to Encourage Immigration into Texas between 1870 and 1890." Master's Thesis, University of Texas, 1955.

McAlister, Samuel B. "The Building of the Texas and Pacific Railroad." Master's Thesis, University of Texas, 1926.

Rickard, John Allison. "The Ranch Industry of the Texas South Plains." Master's Thesis, University of Texas, 1927.

PERIODICALS AND ARTICLES

Crane, R. C. "Early Days in Sweetwater," *West Texas Historical Association Year Book,* VIII (June, 1932), 97–125.

Downing, Jo Dean, comp. "The Story of Midland." Bureau of Business
Research, University of Texas, Austin, Texas, Midland County File.
(Typewritten.)

Drill Bit, 1953–1954.

Gard, Wayne. "The Fence Cutters," *Southwestern Historical Quarterly*,
LI (July, 1947), 1–15.

Holt, R. D. "The Introduction of Barbed Wire into Texas and the Fence
Cutting War," *West Texas Historical Association Year Book*, VI (June,
1930), 65–79.

Hutto, John R. "Big Spring and Vicinity," *West Texas Historical Association Year Book*, VIII (June, 1932), 75–96.

Lang, Aldon Socrates. "Financial History of Public Lands in Texas,"
The Baylor Bulletin, XXXV (July, 1932).

McKitrick, Reuben. "The Public Land System of Texas, 1823–1910,"
Bulletin of the University of Wisconsin, Number 905, (1918).

Oil and Gas Journal, 1920–1958.

West Texas Today, 1928–1958.

Williams, J. W. "A Statistical Study of the Drought of 1886," *West Texas
Historical Association Year Book*, XXI (October, 1945), 85–109.

World Oil, 1930–1955.

World Petroleum, 1950–1954.

NEWSPAPERS

Abilene (Texas) *Reporter News*, 1925–1964.
Amarillo (Texas) *Daily News*, 1940–1964.
Big Spring (Texas) *Daily Herald*, 1928–1964.
Big Spring (Texas) *Herald*, 1904–1928.
Colorado City (Texas) *Record*, 1935–1940.
Dallas Morning News, 1900–1964.
Dallas Times Herald, 1950.
El Paso (Texas) *Times*, 1940–1964.
Fort Worth Star Telegram, 1910–1964.
Houston Chronicle, 1954.
Lubbock (Texas) *Avalanche-Journal*, 1920–1964.
Midland (Texas) *Reporter Telegram*, 1910–1964.
Odessa (Texas) *American*, 1948–1964.
San Angelo (Texas) *Standard-Times*, 1940–1964.
Taylor County (Texas) *News*, 1885–1887.

Texas Spur and Dickens Item, 1919–1920.
Wall Street Journal, 1957.

LETTERS AND INTERVIEWS

Collier, Watt. Interview with C. C. Rister, Colorado City, Texas, December 28, 1948. Rister Oil Collection, Southwest Collection, Texas Technological College.

Fisher, Major General W. P. Letter to Senator Robert S. Kerr, May 19, 1959.

Midland County Agent. Letter to the Bureau of Business Research, University of Texas, Austin, Texas, July 14, 1957.

Van Auken, Mark (El Paso Natural Products Company, Odessa, Texas). Letter to the Bureau of Business Research, University of Texas, Austin, Texas, February 17, 1950.

INDEX

Abilene, Tex.: 38
Adams, George I.: 100
Addis well, South Cowden oil field: 109, 110
Agriculture: development of, 10, 12, 14–15, 160–161; cattle raising supplanted by, 15; combined with cattle raising, 35; introduction of windmill in, 37; fencing and, 37; early crops of, 38–45; affected by drought, 39, 50–51, 54; secondary importance of, before 1900, 47–48; problems of, 48, 94; gains of, 48–49; main crops of, 49; expansion of, 1900–1910, 50; effects of Texas Department of Agriculture on, 50–51; effects of farm groups on, 51–52, 70; prosperity of, 53, 54, 160–161; crop production in, 1917–1918, 54; value of, 55; effects of 1920–1923 recession on, 55; improved methods in, 55; development of, 1900–1930, 65–66; in World War I, 66, 161; in 1920–1930, 66, 161; credit problems of, 66–67; farm tenancy in, 67–69; one-crop practice of, 69; crop experimentation in, 70–71; in Howard County, 75; in Nolan County, 1920–1930, 84; in Scurry County, 87; dominance of, 1900–1930, 94; and related industries, 125, 139–140; importance of, in economy, 139–140, 160; in Ector County, 1940, 157; transportation and water needs of, 161–163; production of, 1900–1930, 169; mentioned, vi, 8, 10. SEE ALSO cattle industry; farmers; farm machinery; farm tenancy; settlers; entries for specific counties; entries for specific crops
Air Force Control and Warning Station M-89, Sweetwater: 141

Alabama and Texas Cattle Co.: 8
Albaugh, Ray A.: 120
Amburgey, J. W.: 31
American Geology: 99
ammonium sulphate: 135
Andersen brothers, cattlemen: 8
Andrews, Tex.: v–vi n.
Andrews County, Tex.: v, 120–121
Appalachian area, oil-bearing region: 96
asphalt: 132
Atchison, Topeka, and Santa Fe Railroad: 80, 81
Atlas Supply Co., Odessa: 127
aviation gasoline: 132

Badger, Tex.: 30
barbed wire: 37
Barber County, Kans.: 11
Basin Pipeline Co.: 130 and n.
Battle of San Jacinto: 17 n.
Baytown, Tex.: 136
Beaumont, Tex.: 99
Bend geological series: 119
Benson Cattle Co.: 8
benzene: 132, 136
Big Spring, Tex.: growth of, 25–28; population of, 26; as trading center, 27; Farmers Institute formed at, 51; Texas Agricultural Experiment Station at, 70–71; importance of, 74; newspapers in, 74; banks in, 74; industry in, 75; unemployment in, 76; water supply in, 76–77; life in, 1900–1920, 77–78; population of, 1910–1930, 78; as agricultural shipping point, 78–79; oil industry in, 79; outcrops near, 98; Iatan–East Howard oil field near, 101, 104; oil refinery in, 107, 110, 132–